THE ISRAELI CAMPAIGN OF 1967

Brigadier Peter Young
D.S.O., M.C.

THE ISRAELI CAMPAIGN 1967

Published by Sapere Books.
24 Trafalgar Road, Ilkley, LS29 8HH
United Kingdom

saperebooks.com

Copyright © The Estate of Peter Young, 1967.
First published by William Kimber and Co. Ltd, 1967.
The Estate of Peter Young has asserted its right to be identified as the author of this work.
All rights reserved.

No part of this publication may be reproduced, stored in any retrieval system, or transmitted, in any form, or by any means, electronic, mechanical, photocopying, recording, or otherwise, without the prior written permission of the publishers.

ISBN: 978-1-80055-963-9.

TABLE OF CONTENTS

PREFACE	7
CHAPTER I CHRONOLOGY	9
CHAPTER I: THE LAND GOD GAVE	11
CHAPTER II CHRONOLOGY	28
CHAPTER II: ISRAEL DELENDA EST	30
CHAPTER III: THE MILITARY BALANCE	42
CHAPTER IV: STRATEGIC BACKGROUND	62
CHAPTER V CHRONOLOGY	76
CHAPTER V: THE MAY CRISIS	79
CHAPTER VI CHRONOLOGY	88
CHAPTER VI: SEA AND AIR	89
CHAPTER VII CHRONOLOGY	104
CHAPTER VII: SINAI REVISITED	105
CHAPTER VIII CHRONOLOGY	130
CHAPTER VIII: JORDAN DISMEMBERED	132
CHAPTER IX: NOISES OFF	156
CHAPTER X CHRONOLOGY	170
CHAPTER X: THE SYRIAN MAGINOT	171
CHAPTER XI CHRONOLOGY	184
CHAPTER XI: THE POWERS IN DISARRAY	185
CHAPTER XII: AFTERTHOUGHTS	201
SELECT BIBLIOGRAPHY	210
ACKNOWLEDGEMENTS	212
A NOTE TO THE READER	214

PREFACE

The time has not yet come to write a history of the Israeli campaign of 1967. We are too near the events of last June to be able to discern precisely what took place. Although the war was very fully reported, especially from the Israeli point of view, much of the detail which a historian requires has not been forthcoming. To take only the most obvious example we have practically no eyewitness accounts of the fighting from anyone who fought on the Arab side. Without fuller knowledge of the fate of Arab units and formations it is difficult to judge their military value, though we can make a fair estimate of their chances should they resort to arms once more.

In this brief *blitzkrieg* the Israelis reached the high water mark of their expansion and won the *Lebensraum* they needed to make their country a tenable enceinte. They did not dream of further conquests. Their dearest wish was to sit round the table with their Arab and Egyptian neighbours and arrive at a lasting settlement.

So far the story is clear enough, but what happens next? Will future historians be able to record that the Arabs, though humiliated by their swift defeat, accepted their territorial losses and abandoned the struggle? Who that has the least knowledge of that proud and ancient race can believe this for one moment? Yet, on the other hand, can one imagine the Israelis quitting the ridge on which Qnaitra stands, Jerusalem, or even Sinai, without a fight? Though Qnaitra is unquestionably Syrian its possession covers the sources of the Jordan waters, a point of prime importance to the economy of Israel. The Jordan and the Suez Canal seem to the Israelis to be no more than their *frontières naturelles*. That there should now be a lasting peace between Arab and Jew is rather less likely than that the Franco-Prussian War, with the transfer of Alsace-Lorraine to Germany, should have led to an enduring accord between her and France.

It follows that a fourth Act to this Palestinian tragedy is yet to be played, and that this book is no more than a military commentary upon Act Three.

It is to be hoped that the powers, and in particular the U.S.A. and the U.S.S.R., may desire to bring about a settlement. But this is little more than a pious wish.

Peter Young
Yateley.

CHAPTER I CHRONOLOGY

c. 1250 B.C.: Canaan. Moses leads the Jews out of Egypt.

538 B.C.: 40,000 Jews return from captivity in Babylon and rebuild the Temple.

63 B.C.: Pompey makes Palestine a Roman tributary.

33 A.D.: The Crucifixion.

70 A.D.: Jewish revolt. Titus destroys Jerusalem. Beginning of the *diaspora*.

73: Capture of Masada.

131: Revolt of Bar Kochba.

570: Mecca. Birth of Mohammed.

632: Death of Mohammed.

732: The Battle of Tours. Charles Martel turns the tide of Arab conquests.

1875: Benjamin Disraeli purchases the controlling shares in the Suez Canal.

1881: Germany. An 'Anti-Semitic League' asks Bismarck to disenfranchise the Jews and put an end to their immigration.

1882: Constantinople. 'The Lovers of Zion' issue a manifesto.

1882: Egypt. Rebellion of Arabi Pasha and beginning of British Protectorate.

1882: Dresden. Anti-Semitic Congress.

1894: The Dreyfus Case.

1896: Theodore Herzl publishes *The Jewish State*.

1897: Basle. The first Zionist conference.

1904: Death of Herzl.

1909: The first *kibbutz* founded at Deganiah.

1914–1918: The First World War.

1916: The Sykes-Picot Agreement.

2 November 1917: The Balfour Declaration.

9 December 1917: Allenby takes Jerusalem.

1920: San Remo Conference. The Palestine Mandate awarded to the British Government.

1921: Jaffa. Anti-Jewish riots.

1924: United States. Immigration laws limit the number of immigrants of all nationalities, by quota.

1929: Jewish Agency for Palestine set up. Anti-Jewish disturbances in Palestine.

1930: The British Government informs the League of Nations that self-government for Palestine is impossible.

1933: Hitler becomes Chancellor of Germany. More anti-Jewish disorders in Palestine.

1936–1939: Arab rebellion in Palestine.

17 May 1939: Palestine White Paper limits Jewish immigration to 75,000 over the next five years.

1939–1945: The Second World War.

1944: Stern Gang murder Lord Moyne.

22 July 1946: Jewish terrorists blow up King David Hotel.

29 November 1947: The United Nations General Assembly agrees on the partition of Palestine.

January 1948: Britain announces that the Mandate will end in May.

8 April 1948: Dir Yasin. Jewish terrorist massacre 254 Arab villagers.

12 April 1948: Sheikh Jarrah, Jerusalem. Arabs massacre 77 Jewish doctors, nurses and students.

14 May 1948: Creation of the state of Israel. U.S.A. give *de facto* recognition.

15 May 1948: End of the Mandate. The Arabs make a general attack on Israel.

17 May 1948: The U.S.S.R. recognize Israel.

CHAPTER I: THE LAND GOD GAVE

And I will give unto thee, and to thy seed after thee, the land wherein thou art a stranger, all the land of Canaan, for an everlasting possession; and I will be their God.

Genesis 17: 8.

And as for Ishmael, I have heard thee: Behold, I have blessed him, and will make him fruitful, and will multiply him exceedingly; twelve princes shall he beget, and I will make him a great nation.

Genesis 17: 20.

At the beginning of the nineteenth century, there were no more than eight thousand Jews in Palestine. To the two and a half million of the Dispersion, it remained only a memory. And to some an uncompelling one. For the Jews of Western Europe were already emancipated communities, many of whose members saw their future in assimilation to Gentile society and some of whom, like Marx's father in Germany and Disraeli's in England, had even accepted Christianity. Only in the great ghetto settlements of European Russia, whence the mass of European Jewry had fled Christian persecution in past centuries, did the memory of a land twice possessed, twice despoiled, but ever promised, still burn bright.

Their condition made the likelihood of its repossession extremely remote. Poor, isolated, unworldly, occasionally frightened and intensely, even superstitiously religious, they knew and could visualise no life outside the ghetto. Nor was persecution frequent or intense enough to make them seek one. 'Next year in Jerusalem', the promise exchanged each year at Passover, had become over the centuries not much more than a ritual incantation. Its fulfilment awaited the coming of the Messiah. And who could say when that would be?

But as the century wore on, it became clear that neither assimilation nor the ghetto could offer either wing of European Jewry a satisfactory future. The very success of the Jews of the Emancipation raised barriers of hostility against them, which increasingly took the form of an ideological anti-Semitism, a cult earliest and most fully developed in Germany. And in Russia, after the assassination of Tsar Alexander II, the regime, seeking a way out of trouble traditional in authoritarian states, deliberately fomented a wave of pogroms. In 1881 alone, the Jews of Russia counted 167 major incidents. And so began a new emigration, at first only as far as the less oppressive West but later, and in greater numbers, to America.

Far more important, however, than this physical displacement was the stirring of a new racial consciousness which in the West took a form chiefly nationalist, in the East mainly religious. There numbers of younger Jews, alarmed lest the appeal of assimilation weaken the practice of orthodoxy, were already planning to put themselves beyond its range by a return to Palestine. They hoped not simply, like some of their forefathers, to find a final resting-place in the Holy City, but to found religious colonies on the land. The movement, to which the renewal of persecution lent urgency, came to be known as 'The Lovers of Zion'. A manifesto, issued by a constituent group at Constantinople in 1882, so exactly catches the flavour of its ideals, so uncannily anticipates the objectives of the future Zionist movement, that it is worth quoting in full:

> To our brothers and sisters in Exile!
> 'If I help not myself, who will help me?'

Nearly two thousand years have elapsed since, in an evil hour, after a heroic struggle, the glory of our Temple vanished in fire and our kings and chieftains changed their crowns and diadems for the chains of exile. We lost our country where dwelt our beloved sires. Into the Exile we took with us, of all our glories, only a spark of the fire by which our Temple, the abode of our Great One, was engirdled, and this little spark kept us alive while the towers of our enemies crumbled into dust, and this spark leapt into celestial flame and shed light on the heroes of our race and inspired them to endure the horrors of the dance of death and the tortures of the *autos-da-fé*. And this spark is again kindling and will shine for us, a true pillar of fire going before us on the road to Zion, while behind us is a pillar of cloud, the pillar of oppression threatening to destroy us. Sleepest thou, O our nation? What hast thou been doing until 1882? Sleeping, and dreaming the false dream of Assimilation. Now, thank God, thou art awakened from thy slothful slumber. The Pogroms have awakened thee from thy charmed sleep. Thine eyes are open to recognise the cloudy delusive hopes. Canst thou listen silently to the taunts and mockeries of thine enemies?... Where is thy ancient pride, thine olden spirit? Remember that thou wast a nation possessing a wise religion, a law, a constitution, a celestial Temple whose wall[1] is still a silent witness to the glories of the past; that thy sons dwelt in palaces and towers, and thy cities flourished in the splendour of civilisation, while these enemies of thine dwelt like beasts in the muddy marshes of their dark woods. While thy children were clad in purple and fine linen, they wore the rough skins of the wolf and the bear. Art thou not ashamed?

Hopeless is your state in the West; the star of your future is gleaming in the East. Deeply conscious of all this, and inspired by the true teaching of our great master, Hillel, 'If I

---

[1] i.e. the Wailing Wall.

help not myself, who will help me?', we propose to form the following society for national ends.

1. The Society will be named 'BILU', according to the motto 'House of Jacob, come, let us go'. It will be divided into local branches according to the numbers of its members.

2. The seat of the Committee shall be Jerusalem.

3. Donations and contributions shall be unfixed and unlimited.

WE WANT:

1. A home in our country. It was given us by the mercy of God; it is ours as registered in the archives of history.

2. To beg it of the Sultan himself, and if it be impossible to obtain this, to beg that we may at least possess it as a state within a larger state; the internal administration to be ours, to have our civil and political rights, and to act with the Turkish Empire only in foreign affairs, so as to help our brother Ishmael in the time of his need.

We hope that the interests of our glorious nation will rouse the national spirit in rich and powerful men, and that everyone, rich or poor, will give his best labours to the holy cause.

Greetings, dear brothers and sisters!

HEAR, O ISRAEL! The Lord our God, the Lord is one, and our land Zion is our one hope.

GOD be with us! THE PIONEERS OF BILU.

Many of these pioneers, materially and morally unequipped for the task of colonisation, quickly succumbed to hardship and disease. Their settlements did not prosper and were saved from extinction only by the philanthropy of western Jewish magnates. A second wave of settlers, who began to arrive in Palestine about 1905, were more successful. Better prepared, more generously financed, they brought with them the idea of the collective settlement (*kibbutz*), at the first of which,

Deganya, Moshe Dayan was to be born in 1915. The dynamic which impelled them was, however, no longer that of a religious minority. For at the end of the eighteen-nineties, the ideal of the Return, now known as Zionism, had suddenly taken fire. Within ten years, it had become an international movement, with funds, organisation, ideology and a programme. In so far as this was the achievement of any one man, he was Theodore Herzl, whose *The Jewish State*, published in 1896, had supplied the spark.

Herzl typified the assimilated western Jew of his generation and background. Neither in Budapest, where he was born, Vienna, where he grew up, nor Paris, where he spent his working life as a distinguished journalist, did he suffer discrimination. No doubt he looked forward to a time when all Jews would be accepted everywhere as easily as he was himself. Like many other Jewish intellectuals, he came eventually to believe this an illusion. His own disillusionment was provoked by the outburst of anti-Semitism released in France by the Dreyfus affair, an anti-Semitism altogether more virulent than the German variety, all the less expected in a society so civilised. If the Jews could not find acceptance there, they could find it nowhere outside a state of their own. That, in short, was the message of the book he dashed off. Its boldness surprised the author. It electrified Jews everywhere, East and West, most of whom, like Herzl, knew nothing of Zionism or, if they did, only what they could glean of it from turgid rabbinical prose. His book leant immediate strength to the scattered Zionist groups. Within a few months it brought them together in a 'World Zionist Organisation'. Next year their representatives assembled at Basle for a Zionist Congress to decide a programme.

The Congress agreed to seek 'the establishment of a home for the Jewish people in Palestine, secured by public law', to be attained successively by colonisation, the organisation and indoctrination of Jews abroad and the achievement of government support. Its imprecise and gradualist flavour reveals it for the compromise that it was. Herzl's argument had been for the immediate acquisition of territory somewhere, somehow, to be colonised forthwith by mass emigration, on the grounds that segregation and nationhood offered the only speedy relief for Jewish disabilities, at a moment when speed seemed essential. He retreated only when convinced that Palestine alone offered a focus of feeling intense enough to unite Jewry behind Zionism — a reasonable retreat which rightly secured him the movement's leadership. And once agreed on Palestine, the Congress was bound to adopt a gradualist programme and substitute the idea of a 'national home' for that of a Jewish state. Palestine, after all, was a province of the Turkish empire, whose ruler besides having the interests of fellow-Moslems to consider was unlikely to tolerate, far less co-operate in, designs to diminish his own sovereignty. Statehood, moreover, was not an aspiration to which all Jews could assent, entailing as it might the suspicion of dual loyalties. Many had already voiced their opposition to it, and would continue to do so, the most strictly orthodox on religious, the best assimilated on cultural grounds.

The 'government support' which the Zionists planned to solicit had, in the first instance, to be that of the Sultan, with whom they now opened negotiations. Herzl, however, was anxious to enlist the support of any power with Mediterranean interests. And so began an extraordinary round of visits — to the Kaiser, the Kings of Italy and Bulgaria, the Tsar's ministers, and last the Pope. All were fruitless, as indeed he might have expected. Later, the Portuguese government was to make an offer of territory in Angola, which some Zionists, impressed by the success of Baron Hirsch's settlements in Argentina, were prepared to take up. The majority rejected it on the grounds that it could never be more than a *Nachtasyl* — a temporary refuge. In the same way they had earlier rejected the British Government's offer of land in Kenya.[2] They still pinned their hopes on winning over the Sultan, not — oddly enough — by appeals to his better nature, but by material inducements — offers of Jewish expertise and promises of money. These were attractive, as was the prospect of building up a racial counterbalance to the disaffected Arab population. None was attractive enough. In 1902, after six years of negotiation, the Sultan countered with a proposal — his last — for the piecemeal settlement of Jewish families (who must become Ottoman subjects and perform military service) in every province of his empire *except* Palestine. This rebuff was not to prevent a renewal of offers by Zionist agents, at the height of Turkey's troubles in the First World War, but these were unashamedly opportunist. It had long been clear that, in normal circumstances, Zionism could not do business with the Sublime Porte.

But the circumstances of the First World War were not normal; for Zionism, they were to prove wholly, even miraculously abnormal. For within three years of its outbreak, and in return for no visible advantage, for no material earnest of reward, the British government was to make the Zionist leaders a firm guarantee of support for the establishment of the national home. It was contained in a letter from Mr Balfour, the Foreign Secretary, to Lord Rothschild:

---

[2] Although this was known as the 'Uganda Scheme' the territory concerned was in what is now Kenya.

Foreign Office,
November 2, 1917

Dear Lord Rothschild,

I have much pleasure in conveying to you on behalf of His Majesty's Government the following declaration of sympathy with Jewish Zionist aspirations, which has been submitted to and approved by the Cabinet:

'His Majesty's Government view with favour the establishment in Palestine of a National Home for the Jewish people, and will use their best endeavours to facilitate the achievement of this object, it being clearly understood that *nothing shall be done which may prejudice the civil and religious rights of existing non-Jewish communities in Palestine*[3] or of the rights and political status enjoyed by Jews in any other country.'

I should be grateful if you would bring this declaration to the knowledge of the Zionist Federation,

yours sincerely,

Arthur James Balfour.

The motives which brought the British government to make this declaration, one must repeat, defy analysis. It was true that in Britain, of all countries, the Jews had been earliest and most fully accepted. It is true that support for Zionism was warm and widespread at many levels. Balfour himself was a sympathiser and, as Prime Minister of the last Conservative administration, had approved the Kenyan offer to the Congress. It is also true that Britain's fortunes were at a low ebb in November 1917 and that her leaders sought support from any quarter. But which so unlikely as the Zionist, a movement with rather less soldiers at its command than the Vatican? The making of the declaration can, in fact, be understood only in terms of personalities: those of David Lloyd George, the instinctual humanitarian, of Herbert Samuel,

---

[3] Author's italics.

the Zionist activist in the Cabinet, of Balfour himself, of Sir Mark Sykes, his adviser on Middle Eastern affairs, and of Dr Chaim Weizmann, by profession a Manchester University lecturer but, since Herzl's death in 1904, the most dynamic of the Zionist leaders. It was his incessant and skilful indoctrination of these others, already sympathetic to his ideals, influentially placed, desperate for remedies and half-ready to believe that world Jewry could supply some, which explain, if anything can, this sudden and well-nigh incredible realisation of Zionist hopes.[4]

But the Zionists were by no means yet home or even half-way there. The Declaration was not an executive instrument. Its implementation was contingent on an Allied victory over Turkey; and must thereafter depend, first, on Allied agreement to include its provisions among those for the general settlement of Turkey's possessions, second, on the satisfaction of Arab interests. For these Britain bore a heavy responsibility. She had encouraged the Arabs to revolt for her own military advantage. She had in return promised her support for the independence of Turkish Arabia to Sherif Hussein of Mecca in 1915. These promises, however, were compromised by a secret Anglo-French agreement (the Sykes-Picot of 1916) to divide control of the richest Arab areas between themselves. As soon as this was made known, as it was by the Bolsheviks in November, 1917, and though both it and the 1915 agreement excluded or seemed to exclude Palestine from their terms, the

---

[4] The common belief that the declaration was a bribe for American Jewish support to bring America into the war is unfounded. The declaration was made seven months *after* America's entry. Some comparison may, however, be drawn with Roosevelt's efforts to bring Russia into the war with Japan. His concessions to Stalin increased in value as the need for Russian assistance diminished.

chance of Arab co-operation in Zionist schemes was very much reduced.

In practice, their co-operation was not to prove necessary. British enthusiasm for pan-Arabism did not survive the victories of 1918; France had never felt any. The post-war dismemberment of the Turkish Empire, though implemented through the mandatory system established by the League of Nations, was effected exclusively in terms of Anglo-French strategic necessities. These — for Britain the security of the Suez Canal, for France that of her Moslem North African possessions — could not be reconciled with the existence of independent Arab states on the Mediterranean shore. It and its hinterland was accordingly divided between them, much along the lines foreshadowed in the Sykes-Picot agreement. France received the Mandate to administer Syria and the Lebanon, with whose Arab Christian population she had traditional ties, Britain that for Iraq, Palestine and Transjordan. Her protectorate over Egypt, which she had exercised since 1882, continued.

Since national self-interest determined the post-war settlement, the British might well have been expected to find their promises to the Zionists as inconvenient as those to the Arabs. Their conquest of Palestine seemed, on the contrary, only to heighten their determination to give them effect. They sought and won the Mandate for Palestine. They had the provisions of the Balfour Declaration included in its terms. And they maintained a large garrison in the country to supervise its institution. The Arabs gave them fair, if inarticulate, warning that trouble lay in store. Lloyd George and Churchill preferred to heed the very much more skilful arguments of the Zionists: that the local Arabs were docile and unpolitical, that they themselves had a working relationship with the Arab leaders and that both conceded Palestine's 'universal character'. The British were reassured; Weizmann's diplomacy was of a higher order than Herzl's. Difficulties of course they foresaw, not least in bringing the country to independence, which the Mandate system bound them to do. What apparently they did not foresee was that, were the other mandated Arab states to achieve their independence more quickly, the continued tutelage of their Palestinian brethren would provide the focus for pan-Arab feelings.

But at the outset, pan-Arabism was no more than a complicating factor in the British mandatory government's problems. These were to find means of reconciling Balfour's twin pledges: to establish a national home for the Jews and to do so without prejudice to the rights of the Arabs. In 1922 the latter numbered about half a million. The majority were peasant farmers, poor and uneducated and many the tenants of absentee landlords. The middle class was small and riven by family factions. An Arab leadership hardly existed; its only effective organ was the Muslim Supreme Council, a purely religious body. By contrast the Jews, though less than a hundred thousand in number, were already highly organised, through the international Zionist Organisation, the Zionist Executive (later Jewish Agency) in Palestine, a statutory body with which the Government negotiated directly and the Histadruth, a conglomerate trade union, political party and social service administration. At Tel Aviv on the coast, they were building a purely Jewish city and in the *kibbutzim* of Galilee they were establishing a distinct and unique way of life, besides reclaiming the land from centuries of abuse and neglect.

British hopes of fostering cooperation between these disparate communities (which also included numbers of

Christian Arabs and anti-Zionist Jews) lay in the device of indirect rule. They planned to establish an elective legislature in which Jews and Arabs would learn to settle their differences by debate and come eventually to assume responsibility for a truly bi-national state. They reckoned without the fundamental attitude of either. The Arabs would not sit in it, except as a majority group, because they were not prepared to further bi-nationalism. The Jews were prepared to sit but were really more concerned to press forward the activities essential to the consolidation of the Home: the expansion of territory and population.

The British were thus forced to exercise the mandate by direct rule in familiar colonial style and to regulate conflicts between the communities by application of the 'economic absorptive capacity' principle. By this was meant that no more Jewish immigrants should be admitted than the Zionists could support and settle, without disappropriating Arabs or robbing them of employment. It was a flabby principle, liable to evasion and subject to pressures beyond the mandatory government's control. For the first years, however, it worked with some success. An economic slump retarded Zionist expansion in the Twenties while the Arabs prospered modestly under mandatory health, welfare and investment schemes. The anti-Jewish disorders of 1919, 1920 and 1921 were not repeated. But the calm was illusory. The balance of population and land tenure was moving steadily in the Jews' favour and with it rose Arab fears of eventual subjugation. By 1928 there were 151,000 Jews in Palestine, by 1932 180,000 and by 1936, after three years' frenzied flight from the new Nazi regime in Germany, almost 400,000. Relations between the two communities, despite the benefits Jewish investment brought the Arabs, had deteriorated; in 1929 and 1933 there had been serious anti-Jewish disorders. The Arabs now resorted to action against the government itself, first through a general strike, then by terrorism. A Royal Commission reported that the Mandate had become unworkable and recommended partition. A further outbreak, in protest against this very limited concession to Zionist nationalism, was not quelled until 1939 and then only after the issue of a White Paper which spelt an effective end to Zionist aspirations: their confinement to a tiny corner of northern Palestine, a limit of 75,000 on future immigration and the grant of Arab independence in the rest of the country within ten years.

The outbreak of war, which bound Zionist and British interests more closely together than ever, prevented any open resistance to the White Paper by the Yishuv — the Jews of Palestine. It brought to a head, however, a growing difference between them and the grandees of international Zionism. As long as Weizmann had carried weight in Whitehall, they had been willing to quell their extremists and co-operate in his gradualist approach. Now, with his Gentile allies dead, retired or distracted, he no longer seemed to do so and they determined to strike out on their own. The official leadership resolved to work openly for nothing short of statehood; the extremists braced themselves to seize it by force.

Force is, of course, the basis on which every state rests, a truth from which most Jews had shied away, as they had hitherto from the challenge of statehood. They were, after all, a race quite without modern military experience or traditions. Even where, in the lands of the Dispersion, Jews were free to make military careers, few had chosen to do so; the fate of Captain Dreyfus was hardly an incentive. A handful had, however, from the earliest moment of Zionism, argued that Jews could not hope to be citizens of a Jewish state without learning to be soldiers: Trumpeldor, a hero of the Russo-Japanese war and martyr of the 1921 Arab uprising, and Jabotinsky, founder of the first purely Jewish unit of Modern times, the Zion Mule Corps of the Gallipoli expedition showed the way. Necessity had driven others to accept their logic; by the 1930's, most *kibbutzim* fielded defence troops, who could trace their origins to the Hashomer of pre-Mandate times and which the Zionist leadership oversaw through the Haganah organisation. During the Arab revolt of 1936–39, the British, officially recognising what they had long known existed, issued arms to these groups and gave them an identity as the Jewish Settlement Police. Some provided recruits for an offensive wing, trained by a passionate Gentile convert, Orde Wingate, and known as Special Night Squads. Haganah was, however, an essentially defensive organisation, both in spirit and equipment. As a Zionist body, it accepted the ban on resistance to the mandatory government imposed by the leadership in September 1939. Others refused to do so, notably the Irgun Zvei Leumi, a Haganah splinter group and heir to Jabotinsky, and the avowedly terrorist Stern Gang.

The function of these dissidents, during the next eight years, was to be that of pacemakers. While Haganah, though running arms and immigrants into the country, abode by the truce during the war, and while individual Jews, impatient at British delays in setting up a Jewish National Army, joined up in the normal way in their thousands, IZL and the Stern Gang pursued independent policies. The former carried on a running campaign with the Arabs. The latter chose to attack British officials, a programme which culminated in the murder of the British resident in Cairo in 1944. Officially, the Zionists condemned these outrages. But as the Yishuv heard, impotent and appalled, of the destruction of European Jewry, these blows against a government which still refused to relax the immigration laws seemed to have a certain wild justice about them.

The realisation, in 1946, that the Labour Party, despite its earlier endorsement of Zionist aspirations, intended to maintain immigration control in all its stringency, quite extinguished whatever restraint the terrorists may still have felt. It was their calculation that a campaign of murder and sabotage would so dishearten the British that they would abandon the Mandate unilaterally and leave the competitors to snatch what they could from the wreck. It was not a bad calculation. The British had already signified their wish to hand the Mandate back to the United Nations, the League's successor. The repressive policies which they were meanwhile compelled to pursue brought them such widespread, intense and unjustified obloquy that they became more and more anxious to depart. In November, 1947, the General Assembly agreed that Palestine should be partitioned and in January, 1948, Britain announced that she would give up the Mandate in May. The terrorists abated their attacks. Their efforts, and those of the very much more powerful Haganah, would now certainly have to be turned against the Arabs, who made it clear that they would allow no scrap of Palestine to pass out of Arab sovereignty. Much had done so, however, in the six months before the British left, in the course of an undeclared war which Arabs from beyond Palestine's frontiers now began to join. At the moment of British departure, this war broke out in earnest, with the simultaneous invasion of five Arab armies — Egyptian, Syrian, Lebanese, Transjordanian and Iraqi.

The outcome belied every expectation. The Jews counted only 15,000 mobile troops, and had no artillery, armour or aircraft. They were able, however, to hold the Arabs off for a month, until the United Nations imposed a truce, by which Israel profited, importing large quantities of Czech and war-surplus arms. This turned the balance, morally if not materially, in their favour and by November, despite a second truce, the Israelis, as they were at last able to call themselves, had secured practically the whole area allotted them in the United Nations partition plan, and something more besides. Only on the front with Jordan had things gone really awry; there the Arab Legion had occupied a large part of the area allotted to the Arabs. From it the Jordanians could overlook almost the whole length of the coastal plain and interrupt communications with Jerusalem. Worst of all, the garrison of the Jewish Quarter of the Old City had been expelled and Zionism had lost touch with the historic centre of Judaism. It was not a loss which many Jews were prepared to accept as permanent. 'Next year in Jerusalem'?

APPENDIX
Joseph Trumpeldor (1880–1920)

One of the most revered heroes in Palestine, Trumpeldor may be little known in non-Jewish circles, but his remarkable career deserves notice. Born in the Russian Caucasus his father spent his life proving that a Jew is no coward, and brought up his son on spartan lines. A few nights each week the young Trumpeldor had to sleep on the bare boards; a few days each month his diet was simply bread and water. In 1902 the young man was called up and joined the infantry and in 1904 requested to be sent to Eastern Siberia with his unit. He lost his left arm during the siege of Port Arthur, but returned to duty and was taken when the fortress fell. During a year's captivity he organised schools for the 500 Jews among the prisoners of war. On his return he was received by the Tsarina and made an officer on the Army Reserve — the first Jew to receive such promotion. While a prisoner he had thought of emigrating to Palestine and in 1912 he did so, and became a farmer. When war broke out in 1914 he volunteered for the British Army, saying: 'I can draw my officer's sword with one hand, can't I?' He was given a command in a volunteer Muleteer Corps which served in Gallipoli. Colonel J. H. Patterson, O.C. Zion Mule Corps, described him as 'the bravest man I have ever seen in my life'. Trumpeldor trained his men under enemy fire 'because that's where they are going to be on missions' and he always led from in front. Back in London he volunteered in 1916 for the Jewish Legion. Since, as a foreigner, he could not hold a commission he enlisted as a private. Returning to Palestine after the war he lived and worked at Tel Hai, a small Jewish border settlement or some 50 souls in the Arab area of Galilee. In 1920 they were besieged for two months and on 1 May 1920 Joseph Trumpeldor was shot in the belly. Stuffing his entrails back into his stomach with his one hand he continued to give his orders, expiring while conducting an orderly retreat to the nearest Jewish settlement. His last words were: 'No matter, it is good to die for our country…' His monument is a roaring lion, carved from the rough stone of the Galilean hills.

CHAPTER II CHRONOLOGY

1945: The formation of the Arab League.

25 May 1950: Tripartite Declaration by France, Britain and United States guarantees frontiers of Middle East States and limits arms flow to them.

1951: Murder of King Abdullah of Jordan.

July 1952: Overthrow of King Farouk of Egypt by the Free Officers Movement.

April 1954: Nasser replaces Neguib as President of Egypt. Britain withdraws from Canal Zone.

September 1955: Russo-Egyptian arms deal.

October 1955: Egypt and Syria set up joint Military Command.

December 1955: Britain and America offer to finance Aswan High Dam.

March 1956: Glubb Pasha dismissed by King Hussein of Jordan.

May 1956: Nasser recognizes Red China.

19 July 1956: American withdraws offer to pay for Aswan.

26 July 1956: Nasser announces nationalization of Suez Canal.

29 October 1956: Israel attacks Egypt.

30 October 1956: Britain and France call upon Egypt and Israel to withdraw from Canal.

2 November 1956: British bombers attack Egyptian airfields.

5 November 1956: Anglo-French forces land in Egypt.

March 1957: The Eisenhower Doctrine enunciated.

February 1958: Syria and Egypt merged as United Arab Republic.

July 1958: Revolution in Iraq.

September 1961: Syria leaves United Arab Republic.

September 1962: Revolution in Yemen. Nasser supplies troops to suppress Royalist reaction.

January 1964: Arab Summit Conference convened to co-ordinate opposition to Israel's diversion of Jordan waters.

CHAPTER II: ISRAEL DELENDA EST

> All your strength is in your union
> All your danger is in discord;
> Therefore be at peace henceforward,
> And as brothers live together.
> *The Song of Hiawatha.* Longfellow.

The defeats of 1948 had a profound effect upon the Arab world. Three years before its six most important states — Egypt, Syria, Iraq, Saudi Arabia, Trans Jordan and Lebanon — had, through their establishment of the Arab League, made the first formal statement of Arab nationalism and taken the first tentative step towards Arab unity. The manifest inability of their governments to further either cause against enemies as few and ill-prepared as the Jews of Palestine boded them ill for the future. For Arab nationalism, despite its dependence on rhetoric and its lack of clear aim, agreed programmes or accepted leaders, was by now a force felt everywhere Arabs dwelt — which was to say wherever men spoke Arabic.

A common language and a majority religion were, however, as many Arabs knew, and more were to discover, no firm foundation for a unified Arab state nor even for common Arab policies. For Arab nationalism was, in 1948, as much an affair of visions and hopes as Jewish nationalism had been forty years before — with the important difference that the obstacles which lay between these hopes and their achievement were imposed as much by the *realpolitik* of existing Arab states as by the policies of alien governments. The Arab world was divided against itself: kingdoms against republics, oil states against states without oil, fertile states against desert, puritan against liberal Muslims. Nor were these divisions simple affairs of blocs. Kingdoms were at issue with each other, oil states with oil states. Saudi Arabia, on the one hand, Jordan and Iraq on the other, all princely regimes, had a traditional dynastic enmity. Iraq and Syria competed for command of the Fertile Crescent. Egypt's assumed primacy among Arabs was resented by the rest.

Internally, too, the states were divided: the Lebanese government was shared uneasily between Muslim and Christian. Iraq harboured a large dissident minority of Kurds. In Syria, openly, and in Egypt, covertly, a complex of political factions was in birth, the most important socialist in character. And these divisions and hostilities were all heightened by the pattern of voluntary and involuntary association with Western powers — Egypt's, Iraq's and Jordan's with Great Britain, Saudi Arabia's with America — which nationalists saw as a perpetuation of mandatory tutelage and resented all the more strongly for the West's recognition of and support for Israel. Acquiescence in these associations, after the humiliating ineffectiveness of their anti-Zionist strategies, inevitably accelerated the decline of the traditional regimes.

For if Arabs could agree on nothing else, they could at least agree that Israel as a state must be extinguished: *Israel delenda est*. Their case could be stated, simply, powerfully, unanswerably: the West had mistreated the Jews; in belated recompense it had supported them in wresting a national territory from its Arab inhabitants. That, in Arab eyes, and not only in theirs, was an extension of injustice. Therefore any Arab government which flinched from or failed in the effort to restore Zionist occupied Palestine to its rightful owners denied its Arab character and forfeited its right to the support of the governed. None had wholly passed the test in 1948. Hence all were at risk.

The earliest to succumb was the Syrian, which in March, 1949 fell to the first of what was to become a succession of military coups. But by far the most significant displacement was to occur three years later in Egypt, the most populous, developed and in every sense — cultural, economic, strategic — the most important Arab country. This, too, was a military coup against what had certainly become the most corrupt and inefficient dynasty in the Arab world — with the possible exception of the theocracy in the Yemen. But the regime with which the army replaced King Farouk's was to follow a course quite different from that which military dictatorships elsewhere had made so familiar. The 'Free Officers' who succeeded to power announced, and were swift to show, that they had done so for ends neither selfish nor reactionary. They championed no particular section of society, nor any group of institutions — not even the army itself — and they stood for no extreme political doctrine. What they sought, naively perhaps but with a fervency which demanded respect, was national regeneration. Their programme was one of unity, economic development and social justice. This did not mean that they shrank from authoritarian measures: their first two years of power were devoted to the extinction of political parties, the emasculation of the trade unions and the replacement of the traditionalist Neguib, whom they had chosen for his acceptability to the reactionary Muslim Brotherhood, by the far more radical Nasser. It did mean, however, that they honestly wished the good of the Egyptian people, in particular of the peasantry, whom sweeping measures of land reform quickly brought to their side.

But it was central to their beliefs that internal reform, no matter how far reaching, could not in itself restore Egyptian self-respect or secure for them the unchallenged leadership of the Arab world, which they so earnestly coveted. It was vital to transform Egypt's international status as well. For at the heart of Arab nationalism burned a fierce resentment of Europe's and America's proprietorial attitude to the Arab lands. America's policy was seen as one of economic exploitation; Britain's as last ditch imperialism; that of France as colonialist; and Russia's as merely opportunist — how else explain her recognition of and support for Israel? Young Arabs had begun to argue that they must be free of all foreign entanglements; that they must, in a newly fashionable phrase, follow the path of neutralism. This held particularly true for Egypt, whose sovereignty was embarrassingly incomplete in three important areas: in the British Canal Zone base, over the Canal itself and in the Anglo-Egyptian Sudan.

If, therefore, the Free Officers were to earn the approval of progressive nationalism abroad, to say nothing of opinion at home, it had as a matter of urgency to extinguish these relics of extraterritoriality. Their first efforts were not wholly successful. Neguib was able to negotiate Britain's withdrawal from the Sudan, but without the desired accession of that state to Egypt: its Arab leaders declared for separate independence. Nasser, on Neguib's downfall, achieved a British withdrawal of force from the Canal Zone but was compelled to allow her to maintain her installations which, since the withdrawal from Palestine and India, provided her most important strategic foothold in the Middle East. The compromise was popular with extremes of opinion in neither country; but at that moment both governments found it unavoidable.

As compromises go, it was to have devastating effects. The removal of an effective British buffer heightened Israel's sense of insecurity, to which Arab guerrilla raids lent a substance that Arab rhetoric might not. It also quashed whatever hopes she might still have entertained of securing rights of passage through the Canal or the Straits of Tiran, her alternative outlet to the Red Sea. The national mood became noticeably more bellicose as a result. At the same time Britain sought means to compensate herself strategically in the Middle East, a desire which America was prepared to endorse. Her growing involvement in Asian security, which the British and the French were clearly less and less able to maintain singlehanded, enjoined an extension of her containment policies eastward along Russia's southern frontiers. A land bridge from NATO's flank in Turkey to friendly Pakistan had become a highly desirable arrangement. In January 1955, these desires were formalised by the signature of the Baghdad Pact between Turkey, Iraq, Pakistan and Britain. It was a development highly displeasing to Russia and Egypt alike and one destined to drive them together. It may account for an increasing Russian interest in Middle Eastern affairs.

Not, however, at once. Britain and America still chose to hope that they could pursue traditional policies in the Middle East without alienating its new leaders, provided they offered sufficiently attractive concessions. And their offer of finance for the Aswan High Dam, a project which all Egyptians were determined to believe would at a stroke free their economy from its single crop basis and transform the country into a modern industrial state, was very attractive indeed. It was made at a moment of heightened tension. Israel had, in February, 1955, reacted to a series of Egyptian sponsored raids from the Gaza strip with a ferocious reprisal. Egypt responded first in

September by announcing that she had arranged to barter cotton for modern Russian arms — a transaction which quite upset the Arab-Israeli strategic balance — and then in October by setting up a joint command with Syria. Britain and America proceeded in December, nevertheless, to a formal offer of finance for the Aswan project. This temporarily stabilised the very erratic course of events in the Middle East.

It was too much to hope, in an area so volatile, that it could do so permanently. Syria remained as unstable as ever, though the general drift of its internal affairs was leftward. Saudi Arabia was at bitter odds with Britain over the ownership of the oil rich Buraimi oasis. Nationalist opposition in Iraq to its membership of the Baghdad Pact was growing and Nuri-es-Said was able to hold it in check only by more and more oppressive measures. An ill-judged British attempt late in 1955 to bring Jordan within its scope merely achieved in March, 1956, the dismissal of Glubb Pasha, symbol of Britain's traditional Arabian presence. Britain incorrectly assumed this to have been at Nasser's instigation. Nasser's current policies might, however, have been designed to mislead. For though in close negotiation with Britain and America to clinch the Aswan deal, he persisted meanwhile in a brand of nationalist rhetoric which cast doubt on his good faith. The truth, perhaps, was that his new-found role as an Arab leader of world stature, co-equal of the grandees of neutralism — Tito, Nehru, Sukarno, patron of the Algerian rebellion, champion of the Palestinian-Arab cause, was proving altogether too exhilarating. Like the Western powers, he had persuaded himself that he could have his cake and eat it.

His recognition in May, 1956, of Communist China was to teach him that he could not. John Foster Dulles reacted in July by withdrawing America's offer of aid for Aswan. A week later

Nasser announced the nationalisation of the privately owned Suez Canal. The chain of events set in motion by Britain's departure from the Canal Zone in 1954 now took on an impetus of its own. At a diplomatic level, Britain, France and America sought to reverse Nasser's coup by organising the Canal's user states into an association which would impose its own terms of passage — an unrealistic scheme ultimately nullified by a Russian veto from the Security Council. At a secret and military level, Britain and France began preparations to repossess the Canal by force.

But another invasion of Egypt was meanwhile in preparation, indeed had been ever since the establishment of the Egyptian-Syrian joint command in October. Israel, once more under the hard headed leadership of David Ben Gurion, had then determined on preventive measures. She had since secretly acquired some of the necessary weapons from France who, in breaking her 1950 agreement with Britain and America to balance arms distribution within the Middle East, could claim as justification its total upset by the Russian shipments. France also felt a need to offset Nasser's support for the Algerian revolution, now in its second year. Already privy to Israel's preparations, France naturally saw advantages in drawing them into a wider scheme. An Israeli drive into Sinai would provide exactly the pretext she and Britain sought to insert their own forces along the Canal banks. The three countries co-ordinated their plans accordingly. Though with varying degrees of frankness: the British inner cabinet did not communicate its foreknowledge of Israel's intentions to its own military advisers.

This, among other factors, was to make the Suez war one of the most curious military operations of modern times. The Allied invading force, whose British contingent at least believed its mission to be the seizure of the Canal by *coup de main*, suddenly found itself charged to 'separate the combatants', by forcing their withdrawal to lines ten miles east and west of the Canal respectively. At the moment this ultimatum was delivered, 30 October, Israeli forces were not yet much beyond their own start lines, which they claimed to have crossed merely to extirpate the nests of Egyptian sponsored guerrillas in the Gaza Strip and the Sinai border area. By the time the Anglo-French force began to land, on 5 November, the Egyptian army in Sinai was already beaten, thanks in part to Allied interdiction of its air bases, and both sides had accepted a UN cease fire resolution. The Canal itself was solid with block ships from Port Said south to Suez. Such opposition as the Allies encountered was offered chiefly by hastily armed civilians.

Under Russian threats of retaliation and far graver warnings by America of her intention to withdraw support for the hard pressed pound sterling, the operation petered out almost as suddenly as it had begun. Israel, guaranteed UN supervision of the Straits of Tiran and the Sinai border — from the Egyptian side — withdrew inside her own territory. By December, the last Anglo-French contingents had left Egypt. But if Suez, as a military undertaking, was ludicrous — always excepting Moshe Dayan's glittering thrust across the desert — its political consequences were momentous. It destroyed the last vestiges of British and French influence for good in the Middle East. It achieved the downfall of the British Prime Minister and immersed his successor in the bitterest political crisis since the General Strike. It hardened French determination to prosecute its war with the Algerians *à outrance* — and hence helped to procure the overthrow of the Fourth Republic. It confirmed Israel's belief in the fruitfulness of violence. It imposed on

America the need to further her policies in the Middle East by direct action, not through that of European intermediaries. It ushered in Russia as the Arabs' principle foreign champion and so threatened to bring her face to face with America in yet another corner of the uncommitted world. Finally, and perhaps most importantly, it elevated Nasser to a position of unchallenged primacy among Arab leaders.

For by an extraordinary reversal, Nasser as victim proved an even more compelling symbol of Arab nationalism than Nasser as hero. The two characters, indeed, merged into one and Nasserism, as an unfriendly West now began to describe its dynamic, seemed to know no limits to its influence. The Eisenhower doctrine, by which in March, 1957, America proclaimed its readiness to support any Middle Eastern state which considered its security threatened by Communism offered by contrast a very flimsy refuge for dissenters. Those who appeared to invoke its operation, like King Hussein of Jordan in April, 1958, or President Chamoun of the Lebanon in July, dangerously compromised the viability of their regimes. Those who sought to oppose the spread of Nasserism singlehanded — bourgeois nationalists in Syria, feudal despots in Iraq — merely achieved their own downfall. In February, 1958, Syrian socialists forced a merger of their country with Egypt in a United Arab Republic, shortly, if anomalously, extended by the accession of the Yemen; and in July, the Iraqi monarchy, whose position the Nasserite nationalists had hopelessly eroded, was overthrown by a military coup.

In the midsummer of 1958 then, the Arab Middle East seemed to tremble on the brink of unity under Egyptian leadership. It is, however, from that moment that one is able to date the beginnings of Nasser's decline from primacy. It was marked, first, by a disappointment of expectations that Iraq would join the UAR. Brigadier Kassem quickly showed that he was not prepared to surrender leadership of his own revolution, which was as different in spirit from Nasser's as Iraq was in character from Egypt. Secondly, the union with Syria began to go badly almost from the outset. All attempts to unify the two countries merely served to emphasise their economic and political dissimilarity and to demonstrate the irrelevance of Nasserism to Syrian affairs. A growing sense of second class citizenship provoked the Syrians in September, 1961 to dissolve the union. Pan-Arabism had scarcely gained by its short and uneasy existence. Thirdly, in 1962, Egypt was drawn into a civil war in the Yemen. The campaign was to demand eventually the commitment of 60,000 of her best soldiers, was to bring her no military and very little political honour and was to give her the worst of the odds in an indirect conflict with Saudi Arabia, which supported the deposed monarchy.

Egypt's internal troubles typified those which beset most Arab states as the 1960's drew on. Syria and Iraq each relapsed into internal faction-fighting which culminated in the triumph of their Ba'ath Socialist parties over communist and nationalist rivals in early 1963. Algeria underwent a military coup. The Saudi Arabian monarchy changed hands within the family. This disturbed pattern was accompanied by a marked loss of regional cohesion. Iraq's frustrated attempt to annex Kuwait in 1961 led to her breaking relations with all states which recognised Kuwait's independence. The overthrow of Kassem, which seemed to offer hopes of restoring good Iraqi-Egyptian relations and even of refounding and enlarging the UAR, foundered on fundamental ideological differences between Nasser and the Ba'athists of Syria and Iraq who shortly fell out between themselves. Egypt's indirect conflict with Saudi

Arabia in the Yemen intensified. Even the three new states of the Arab west — Tunisia, Morocco and Algeria — found cause for disagreement. In late 1963, it was calculated that only three of the thirteen member states of the Arab League, Libya, the Sudan and Kuwait, were on satisfactory terms with all the others.

The only issue on which the Arabs were able to muster a show of unity occurred at the end of 1963, when Israel disclosed final details of her long laid plan to divert the upper waters of the Jordan and that unity was short lived, the Arabs proving unable to agree over the division of the waters in a counter-scheme of their own. The series of Arab summit conferences which followed the one called to meet this emergency achieved little more than negative, anti-Israeli gestures — the formation of a Palestine Liberation Army among the refugees of the Gaza Strip and West Bank Jordan and the earmarking of national contingents for joint operations under a united Arab command. The last, scheduled for September, 1966, was cancelled for lack of support.

The Jordan waters dispute is, however, directly connected with the sudden eruption of the crisis of May, 1967. For the states most threatened by Israel's scheme — Jordan and Syria — were those most dependent on Egypt's military power to lend force to their objections. At the outset her involvement in the Yemen precluded her offering anything more than promises. But while these lingered unfulfilled, both states had the strongest possible excuse for condoning, even encouraging, increased guerrilla activity against Israel. Jordan was in practice unwilling to do so, since the guerrillas were drawn from those groups most hostile to the monarchy. She could not, however, prevent Syrian agents from using her much longer frontier with Israel for their penetrations.

Israel's method of reply to the guerrilla campaign was well-established and well known. She allowed a number of incidents to accumulate and then inflicted an exemplary reprisal. These operations, besides having salutary results, served a similar purpose to Britain's imperial frontier campaigns. They blooded recruits and rehearsed commanders. Their effect was, however, arbitrary and indiscriminate. For while the chief support for the guerrillas came from Egypt, her frontier was closed to them by the patrols of the United Nations Emergency Force, to which Nasser apparently wished to give no cause for complaint. Jordan had come to find the situation increasingly intolerable. For Egypt, in effect, reaped all the advantages of an anti-Israel shadow war without suffering any of the penalties. Protected by the blue helmets of the UN, she was at liberty to assault Israel with words, vilify her Arab enemies for faint-heartedness and transfer her military force for her own ends elsewhere.

For Egypt the danger was that she be caught out in her operation of this double standard. For if enmity for Israel was one sentiment which all Arabs could share, laxity in its prosecution had become the cardinal Arab sin. Now that all progressive Arab states, and Egypt above all, bristled with Soviet arms, military weakness could not be pleaded in mitigation. The taint could be expunged only by action. In the event of a major Israeli affront, the divided legions of the United Arab Command would look to their Egyptian chiefs for a lead. Dare Nasser fail to respond?

CHAPTER III: THE MILITARY BALANCE

'Our commanders are wonderful — they are daring and ready to do anything. And the soldiers are wonderful — these soldiers who in ordinary life may be shopkeepers or teachers and the next day can attack like devils. I don't know how to explain it, and I haven't been able to explain it since I started in the Army during the War of Independence as a Platoon Commander, and then became Brigade Commander in the Sinai Campaign, and now Division Commander; but there is something in this nation's spirit which makes it possible.'

Aluf Ariel Sharon.
12 June 1967.

The Sinai Campaign of 1956 left Israel's strategic problems unsolved. Syria and Jordan had contrived to keep out of the fight. There had been no pretext either for the occupation of Qnaitra or the overrunning of the West Bank of the River Jordan. In consequence of a *diktat* from or a deal with Mr. Eisenhower, Sinai and Sharm-el-Sheikh had been evacuated. Israeli frontiers were once more those of 1948 and her strategic situation once more was far from brilliant, and so it was to remain for the next ten years.

The strategic situation before the campaign of June 1967 may be summarized in this way. Israel with a population of 2,500,000 including 300,000 Arabs was surrounded on three sides by more or less hostile neighbours and on the fourth by the Mediterranean Sea which she did not command.

LAND FRONTIERS IN KILOMETRES

Egypt: 300 (186 miles approx.)
Jordan: 530 (385 miles approx.)
Syria: 70 (43 miles approx.)
Lebanon: 85 (53 miles approx.)

POPULATIONS IN MILLIONS

Egypt: 30
Jordan: 2
Syria: 5.5
Lebanon: 1.9
Iraq: 7.5
Saudi Arabia: 5
Total: 51.9

Even Israel's central position — 'interior lines' — seemed to be greatly weakened by the 'wasp waist' of only 14 kilometres between Tulkarm and the sea. It was not impossible for Jordanian artillery near Qalqilya to shell targets in the Tel-Aviv area.

Jerusalem, the seat of the Knesset, Israel's Parliament, was reached by a corridor only seven kilometres wide.

The greatest concentrations of population and industry were dangerously close to the frontiers:

Haifa: Population: 12½%, Industry: 15%, Distance from frontier: 40km
Tel-Aviv area: Population: 37%, Industry: 51%, Distance from frontier: 20km
Jerusalem: Population: 8%, Industry: 5%
Beersheba: Population: 6%, Industry: 4%, Distance from frontier: 50km

Still more serious were the military implications of time and space in the air. Some examples of the time required for a jet plane to reach targets in Israel are significant:

Cairo–Tel Aviv: 35 minutes
Suez Area–Tel Aviv: 20 minutes
Mafraq–Tel Aviv: 10 minutes
Damascus–Haifa: 9 minutes
El Arish–Tel Aviv: 9 minutes

It scarcely seemed a situation in which a country could want war, yet, given the continued hostility of the Arabs, and especially the Syrians, the temptation to seek a swift and bloody solution was ever present, and the more so since, despite her own obvious weaknesses all her neighbours, with the exception of Egypt, were, taken singly, very much weaker than Israel. Arab disunity was one of the strongest factors working for Israel.

The considerations or principles which governed the structure of the Israel Defence Forces were the maintenance of a force to deter potential Arab aggression; the need to achieve *quick* victory in the event of war; stubborn defence of the borders — since there was nowhere to retreat to; the exploitation and integration of the entire national potential into the war effort; the maintenance of both the standing and reserve armies at the highest possible level of readiness; and the minimizing of the burden upon the National Economy.

Given the strategic situation already described, it follows that the key to Israel's defence is command of the air. Her Air Force seems to have consisted of little more than 300 combat aircraft, of all types:

Light bombers: 25 *Vautour* and 48 *Skyhawk*[5]

Interceptors: 72 *Mirage* III-C and 20 *Super Mystère*
Fighter-bombers: 45 *Mystère* IV and 50 *Ouragan*[6]
Trainers: 60 *Magister*[7]
Total: 320

In addition there were:

About 20 *Noratlas* and *Stratocruiser* transports.
25 Helicopters, including S-58 and *Alouettes*.
Some light aircraft, including *Piper Cubs*.
2 battalions of *Hawk* surface-to-air missiles.

The total strength of the Air Force was about 8,000. Although its aircraft were largely French its traditions, in a sense, were those of the R.A.F. — even, one might say, of 'the Few' of 1940. To take only one example Aluf Ezer Weizman, for eight years commander of the Israeli Air Force, had begun his career in the R.A.F. Beyond question the pilots were 'keen types' and had the edge on their Egyptian opponents, who besides being temperamentally somewhat unenterprising were less well able to operate sophisticated equipment.

There had been recent clashes with the Syrian and Jordanian aircraft — in November 1966 for example when the Israelis made a reprisal raid on Samu in Jordan. The results had given the Israelis confidence that they could 'hack the enemy out of the sky'. There had been no recent contact with the Egyptians for the very good reason that their planes never came near the Armistice Line whether by accident or design. The Israelis, somehow or other, had managed to acquire air photographs of every SA-2 site in the Canal Zone … and the present writer

---

[5] Possibly not operational.
[6] Obsolescent.
[7] Can be armed.

saw them in Tel Aviv in October 1966. Beyond question the Israeli Air Force was a well-trained, determined and aggressive organization.

The Israeli Navy, though it was to play its part in the reoccupation of Sharm-el-Sheikh, was very much the junior partner in the I.D.F. With a total strength of 3,000 regulars it manned:

   3 destroyers[8]
   1 anti-aircraft frigate
   3 submarines[9]
   8 MTBs
   3 landing craft

In addition there was a 'frogman commando' specially trained by Yochai Bin-Nun, a former commander-in-chief of the Israeli Navy.[10]

The Israeli Army, fully mobilized numbered about 264,000.

   22 infantry (motorized) brigades. 4,500 strength.
   8 armoured brigades. 3,500 strength.
   1 parachute brigade. 4,000 strength.

Israel had something like 800 tanks:

   250 Centurions
   200 Super-Shermans

---

[8] Including the former *Ibrahim-el-Awal*, captured from the Egyptians in 1956.
[9] The *Rahaf*, being somewhat ancient, could no longer submerge.
[10] David Leitch: *How Israeli frogmen commandos brought sudden death to Nasser's navy. The Sunday Times*, 25 June 1967.

200 M-48 Pattons
150 AMX-13

Comparing the Israeli armour and that of the Egyptians and Syrians, Aluf A. Tal, Commander of the Armoured Corps said (12 June 1967):

> We never laboured under the illusion that we would be able to build up an armoured force equal in numbers or surpassing the Egyptian armour. But we tried to have superiority in quality, and again to obtain this superiority not in equipment but in the men who drive the tanks. For clearly, as to numbers of tanks and their quality, the enemy was always ahead.
>
> We used old tanks, including tanks dating from the Second World War. The enemy ... has the most modern tanks, sometimes acquired even before they are introduced into the Soviet divisions. We tried to improve our tanks, the old tanks, by improvisation, endeavouring to get a better driving gear and better guns. But in any case we cannot improve our tanks so that they can compare or compete with the most modern tanks the enemy has. Even the tanks which have been sold to us during the last few years are not of the most modern type, but are tanks which have become obsolete in the western armies.
>
> The only area where we really can compete is the very narrow domain of human quality and human superiority. This is based first of all on the basic qualities of our youth, which is excellent and fearless.

As to artillery the Israelis had 250 SP guns, including 155mm howitzers on *Sherman* chassis. Their anti-tank weapons included the 106mm recoilless rifle mounted on a jeep, and the SS-10 and SS-11 missiles mounted on weapons carriers.

Besides the 31 brigades there were separate regional defence units in the border areas. Frontier *Kibbutzim* and *Nahal* settlements were sited tactically and organized for all-round defence. Men and women alike were liable for military service.

The strong points of the I.D.F. were its thoroughly competent, and professional officer corps, a highly efficient intelligence system and a mobilization scheme capable of deploying its full potential in something like 48–72 hours. A striking feature was that senior officers, even men of the calibre of General Dayan, were permitted to retire in their forties. The youthfulness of the high commanders was no small factor in the successes of the I.D.F. in 1956 and 1967.

With all its obvious virtues the I.D.F. was a decided shock to an officer trained in the British Army. After a visit to it in October 1966 the present writer recorded his impressions.

> The I.D.F. — consisting of warriors rather than soldiers — makes little or no concession to the ceremonial side of soldiering. A salute is a greeting rather than a drill movement; turnout — except among the numerous and decorative Amazons — is decidedly individualistic, and shaving though permitted, is not of daily occurrence. But one never sees a dirty weapon.[11]

THE UNITED ARAB REPUBLIC

Their officers are too fat, and their soldiers are too thin.
Chaim Weizmann.

The Egyptian is a good soldier, a disciplined soldier, but I think the commanders are very poor. I would not trust them. We do not think they have any fighting spirit. They are very good where everything is very simple; they are well organized, and they are very good at shooting. I must tell you a story about something that happened 12 years ago. We

---

[11] The *Daily Telegraph*. 15 November 1966.

attacked an Egyptian battalion ... at Sabba near Nitzana, and managed in a few minutes to destroy the position. Then, a few weeks later, we attacked the Syrians ... and we put the prisoners together... The Syrians asked the Egyptians how it could have happened that a battalion in a fortified defensive position, mined, and having artillery, was defeated in a few minutes. The Egyptians answered: 'Those Jews don't attack according to the book.'

Aluf Ariel Sharon

The Egyptian Air Force had been entirely equipped by the U.S.S.R. These are the details:

Total strength: 20,000; *c.* 450 combat aircraft.
36 Tu-16 medium jet bombers.
40 Il-28 light jet bombers.
100–120 MiG-21 C/D jet interceptors.
80 MiG-19 all-weather fighters or fighter-bombers.
200 MiG-15, MiG-17 and Su-7 fighter bombers.
About 60 transports, including Il-14 and An-12.
60 helicopters including 8 Mi-6 *Hook*.
Training aircraft, some of which could be armed, made up another 120 aircraft.

Air Defence was provided both by conventional anti-aircraft guns, and by 150 SA-2 *Guideline* surface-to-air missiles deployed in 25 batteries of 6 launchers each. These missiles were supported by a recently-installed radar network and by the six squadrons of MiG-21 interceptors.

This was a formidable array of weaponry, but nothing in the history of the Egyptian Air Force suggested that the aircraft were manned by pilots imbued with an aggressive and enterprising spirit.

The organization of the Navy was:

Total strength: 11,000.
8 destroyers (6 ex-Soviet *Skory* class, 2 ex-British 'Z' type).
11 submarines (ex-Soviet 'W' class).
6 escort vessels.
6 coastal escorts.
18 missile patrol boats (10 *Osa* class, 8 *Komar* class, both with *Styx* short-range cruise missiles).
10 minesweepers.
About 50 small patrol vessels.

The *Osa* and *Komar* class patrol boats were equipped with missiles, capable of sea to ground attack. With her long coastline and 'wasp-waist' Israel seemed vulnerable to attack from the sea by rockets.

The organization of the Egyptian Army was:

Total strength: 180,000 (including mobilized reservists).
2 armoured divisions (with 350 medium and heavy tanks each).
4 motorized rifle divisions (with about 150 medium tanks each).
1 parachute brigade.
12 artillery regiments.
About 1,200 tanks and assault guns, including 350 T-34, 500 T-54 and T-55, 60 JS-3 and 150 Su-100.
100 surface-to-surface missiles with ranges of between 200 and 450 miles were not believed to be operational on 4 June 1967.
Army reserves totalled a further 60,000. There was a paramilitary National Guard of about 60,000.

The army in the Yemen had probably been reduced to under 50,000 men. The Palestine Liberation Army (P.L.O.) consisting of about 30,000 irregular troops trained by the Egyptians was stationed mostly in the Gaza Strip.

On paper this was a formidable force. According to Aluf S. Gavish (Israeli Southern Command) there were seven Egyptian divisions in Sinai when the June campaign began.

> Two were armoured divisions; one was a division of Palestinians in the Gaza Strip, which was the 20th Division; the 7th Division was situated between Rafiah and El Arish; the 2nd Division was positioned along the Abu Agueila-Qusema line; the 3rd Division along the Jebel Libni-Bir Hasna line; the 4th Armoured Division was between Bir Gafgafa and Bir Temedeh; the 6th Infantry Division was stationed between Nakhl and Quntyileh; and a special armoured force of division size was in the Qreya Pass facing Mitzpe Ramon.[12]

There were concrete fortifications — for example at Sheikh Zuwaib and Jirdi covering El Arish — and in general the Egyptian position has been described as 'stretching back in depth in both directions for 12 kilometres, with fortified positions on each side including anti-tank guns, tanks and mines.'

In effect the Egyptians had behaved rather as Marshal Graziani did in Libya in 1940 when he advanced in great strength to the Egyptian front, constructed a fortified position, and, by deliberately surrendering the strategic initiative, challenged the British to try and oust him.

JORDAN

---

[12] Press Conference of 12 June 1967.

I believe the Arab tribesman to be first-class military material. I am convinced that they are the same men who conquered half the world 1,300 years ago. To the world at large, however, they are still unknown. They have not had the opportunity to prove themselves on a major battlefield. If they had done so, they would have emerged with fresh self-confidence, and with the respect of the world — a state of affairs which would have been better for both.

Glubb Pasha, 1948

'Al harb al yom ma biha leddha'
(There is no joy in war nowadays)[13]

Za'al ibn Mutlaq, 1941

To those of us who knew and loved the Arab Legion there can be only regret that given the chance to display its prowess in modern warfare the Jordan Arab Army should have met with shattering defeat in a bare three days.

It is easy to say 'this would never have happened if King Hussein had not sacked his British officers'. And it is true that not all the 'reforms' that followed the events of March 1956 seem to the present writer to have been well-judged. But the essential truth of the matter is very simple. Even with Iraqi backing, the forces of Jordan, and especially her Air Force, were not strong enough to try conclusions with Israel.

Jordan's Air Force, despite the keen interest which King Hussein took in it, was minute.

Total strength: 2,000.
12 *Hunter* Mk. 6 fighter/fighter-bombers.
16 *Vampire* Mk. 9 fighter-bombers.
F-10s were believed not to be operational.

---

[13] From *The Story of the Arab Legion*, pp. 325 and 355.

The Jordanian Navy — in former times its British commander was known as 'The Dead Sea Lord' — consisted of a few patrol and landing craft in the Dead Sea and the Gulf of Aqaba.

The Jordan Arab Army, though it had expanded rapidly since 1956, was less than one-third the size of the Israel army, and had a frontier of 530 kilometres to defend.

    Total strength: 55,000.
    6 infantry brigades.
    3 armoured brigades.
    250 tanks, including 150 M-48 *Pattons*. Also some Centurion tanks and 155mm howitzers.

Even with the support of one of the five Iraqi divisions there was going to be little left as a *masse de manoeuvre* once the key points on the West Bank had been garrisoned.

The weakness of Jordan's position was, therefore, that she depended for air cover upon the Egyptians.

The old pre-1956 Arab Legion consisted of three infantry brigades and an armoured arm of one tank and two armoured car regiments. There were three field regiments and a LAA regiment as well as engineers and signals. The men were keen long-service soldiers, and their training was improving by leaps and bounds. Some of the infantry regiments were very good and so was the field artillery. It would be wrong to pretend that all units were devoted to the Hashemite Kings. The engineers and signals were particularly disaffected. From the internal security point of view the fact that five infantry and two armoured car regiments were Bedouin was a great strength to the throne.

While there were many good officers, there was a distinct shortage of potential battalion and company commanders. With triple expansion one wonders where all the officers have sprung from. On the other hand one could hardly wish for better platoon and section commanders than some of those who gave me their support in the 9th Regiment of the Arab Legion. Where are they now?

Dr. Adair, a member of my Department, who, when a National Service subaltern in the Scots Guards, served with me in Jerusalem long ago, visited Jordan last year and I quote his perceptive comments:

> The Jordanian Arab Army had both changed and yet remained in many ways the same as the Arab Legion I left in 1955. The increased size, the American transport and small arms (we saw no tanks), the abolition of the predominantly Bedouin regiments, the great emphasis on education in the officer's career, the extreme political consciousness of the officer cadets and the varying abilities of the officers I met (ranging in my subjective judgment from some very fine ones by any standards to a few very doubtful starters): These are some of the impressions I carried away with me. Unfortunately we saw too little of the Army on training to form any but the most superficial opinions of its efficiency and effectiveness in the field.

Training: there's the rub. Not all Arab officers care much for training. There are those who prefer to sit and drink coffee and listen to Egyptian broadcasts…

SYRIA

Morale appeared high but the most worrying thing, militarily, is the calibre of officer and non-com. These have been purged so often that only the lowest-born peasant seems to be considered leadership material.

Colin Simpson.[14]

---

[14] In the *Sunday Telegraph*, 4 June 1967.

The Syrian forces with 120 Russian combat aircraft was considerably stronger than the Jordanian, but her army was weaker, both in numbers and in quality than that of King Hussein.

Air Force
Total strength: 9,000 men; 106 combat aircraft.
6 Il-28 light bombers.
20 MiG-21 jet interceptors.
20 MiG-19 jet interceptors.
60 MiG-17 fighter-bombers.
Transports, trainers and helicopters.

The Syrian Navy played no great part in the struggle.

Total strength: 1,500.
6 coastal escorts.
2 minesweepers.
4 missile patrol boats (*Komar* class).

The Syrian army, which could claim that it had not been defeated by the Israelis in 1948 or 1956, was distinctly 'Maginot-minded'. It had had 20 years in which to fortify the rocky but 'tankable' slopes that lead up from the Huleh valley to the plateau round Qnaitra. Here five of its nine brigades were deployed on a 43-mile front. In October 1966 I was able to reconnoitre this position from the west, and got just as good a look at it as any battalion commander might expect on the eve of an attack. These were my impressions:

> Although their layout may owe something to German or Russian influence its real model is the Maginot line system — without the forts. There is the old three-line system, *Ligne de Contact, Ligne de Recueil, Ligne d'Arrêt*, familiar to those of the B.E.F. who had their Baptism in the Saar in 1940... Many of

the pillboxes and defensive positions can easily be seen without a telescope. The 'going' is not very good by reason of numerous boulders, but despite the high ground the position does not appear particularly formidable.[15]

Just before the fighting began in June 1967 Colin Simpson (The *Sunday Telegraph*) visited the area and reported:

> The Syrian Army is badly disciplined and weapons are filthy, I did not see one position sited for all-round defence and with the exception of a few carefully-sited emplacements, fields of fire were limited and not interlocking.

The army was probably too thin on the ground to have an absolutely continuous front.

> Total strength: 50,000.
> 2 armoured brigades.
> 7 infantry brigades.
> About 400 Soviet tanks, of which only 200 were operational.
>   Soviet artillery up to 155mm.
> 10 SA-2 *Guideline* sites.

It may be worth noting that the Syrian artillery was considered by the Israelis (October 1966) to be efficient. It was thought that they had the benefit of Russian instruction.

In support of the Syrian 'Maginot Line' there was the 70th Tank Brigade with Russian T.54s. Simpson also saw one T.55. There was another tank brigade in lager on the Homs road, either as a mobile reserve or ready to hold Damascus.

It was thought, rather questionably, that the only possible avenue of approach for Israeli armour was near the Lebanese

---

[15] Brig. Peter Young: 'View from Beleaguered Israel'. The *Daily Telegraph*, 15 November 1966.

border and by the River Banias. Here the Syrians had deployed anti-tank guns in depth, each gun having several alternative positions.

IRAQ

Although Iraq could only be expected to spare something like one division to support Jordan, the intervention of her reasonably powerful Air Force was foreseen by Israel.

> Total strength: 10,000 men. *c.* 170–200 combat aircraft including:
> 10 Il-28 jet bombers.
> 60 MiG-21 interceptors.
> 50 *Hunter* Mk. 9 ground-attack.
> 30 MiG-17 and MiG-19 jet fighters.
> 20 T-52 jet *Provost* light strike.
> 2 Wessex helicopter squadrons.
> About 40 Soviet and British medium transports.

The Iraqi Navy — a small number of MTBs and patrol vessels — was not expected off the coasts of Israel.

The Army, most of which was required for internal security at home numbered:

> Total strength: 70,000.
> 1 armoured division.
> 4 infantry divisions.
> About 600 tanks, of which 400 were operational: mostly T-54 and T-34 with some *Centurions*.
> 5 batteries SA-2 *Guideline* missiles.

SAUDI ARABIA

Saudi Arabia played virtually no part in the brief campaign, but her forces had to be taken into account by the I.D.F. at the planning stage. Her weakness in the air was one factor which made her intervention somewhat unlikely.

> Total strength: 5,000, about 20 combat aircraft.
> 6 *Hunter* and 6 *Lightning* jet fighters (with British mercenary pilots).
> 12 obsolescent F-86 *Sabre* jet fighters.
> About 40 transports and trainers.
> Some *Thunderbird* surface-to-air missiles were being installed around airfields.
>
> *Navy*
> Total strength: 1,000.
> Coastal patrol craft only.
>
> *Army*
> Total strength: 30,000.
> About 5 infantry brigades of which two were kept for internal security purposes.
> A few M-24 light tanks.

It is obvious that Saudi Arabia was at this period very far from having developed her full military potential.

LEBANON

Although some Fatah raids into Israel had been carried out from Lebanese territory, there was no doubt in Israeli minds that Lebanon meant to live in peace. A glance at the military strength of Lebanon is sufficient to confirm this view.

> *Air Force*
> Total strength: 1,000 men; 18 combat aircraft.
> 12 *Hunter* jet fighters.
> 6 *Vampire* jet fighter-bombers.

10 *Alouette* helicopters.

Navy
Coastal patrol craft only.

Army
Total strength: 12,000.
8 infantry battalions.
2 tank battalions.
40 *Centurions* and 40 AMX-13 tanks.
155mm French artillery.

SUMMARY

Israel Strength
Combat Aircraft: 320
Tanks: 800
Deployed Manpower: 264,000

Combined Arab Strength
Combat Aircraft: 752
Tanks: 1,650+
Deployed Manpower: c.300,000[16]

It is interesting to note that though the Israelis were outnumbered by at least two to one in planes and tanks, they could, thanks to their excellent mobilization scheme, hope to make much better use of their manpower, not that mere numbers count for much in modern warfare.

THE ARMS RACE

None of the powers engaged in the campaign of June 1967 was

---

[16] Less garrisons in Egypt and the expeditionary force in the Yemen.

capable of producing its own planes, tanks or warships. These were obtained from the U.S.S.R., the U.S.A., France or Great Britain. Before the First World War the morality of selling arms was seldom if ever questioned, but in the thirties one heard a great deal — especially from American isolationists — as to the evils of 'the Arms Racket'. The fact seems to be that sovereign states, incapable of producing their own weapons, will purchase them from a foreign power, and that being so it is merely a question of commerce. If the U.S.A. will not provide the U.S.S.R. will. If the performance of a British tank seems more efficient than that of a Russian one there will be no tears shed in Whitehall, Lulworth or the Vickers-Armstrong works. But, of course, it is not as simple as all that. There is an element of 'cock-fighting' in the whole business. The big gamblers provide the spurs and lay their wagers. One of the cocks gets savaged; one of the gamblers has to give up the game or produce another stake. At least the principals have not come to blows.

WHO PROVIDED WHAT

U.S.A.
For Israel:
48 *Skyhawks*.
200 *Super-Shermans*.
200 M-48 *Pattons*.
For Jordan: 150 M-48 *Pattons*.
For Saudi Arabia: 12 *Sabres*.

U.S.S.R.
For U.A.R.:
476 combat aircraft.
25 SA-2 batteries.
6 destroyers.

18 missile patrol boats.
c. 1200 tank and assault guns.
For Syria:
106 combat aircraft.
10 SA-2 sites.
4 missile boats.
c. 400 tanks.
For Iraq:
Some T-54 and T-34 tanks.
5 SA-2 batteries.

FRANCE
For Israel:
272 combat aircraft.
150 AMX-13 tanks.
For Lebanon: 40 AMX-13 tanks.

GREAT BRITAIN
For Israel: 250 *Centurions*.
For U.A.R.: 2 'Z' type destroyers.
For Jordan:
28 combat aircraft.
Some *Centurions*.
For Iraq:
50 *Hunters*.
Some *Centurions*.
For Saudi Arabia:
12 combat aircraft.
For Lebanon:
18 combat aircraft.
40 *Centurions*.

It would appear that armaments manufacturers show a remarkable impartiality in distributing their hardware — and none more impartial than the British.

CHAPTER IV: STRATEGIC BACKGROUND

'You will observe the Rules of Battle, of course?' the White Knight remarked, putting on his helmet too.

'I always do,' said the Red Knight, and they began banging away at each other with such fury that Alice got behind a tree to be out of the way of the blows.

'I wonder, now, what the Rules of Battle are,' she said to herself, as she watched the fight, timidly peeping out from her hiding-place:...[17]

We have seen what ironmongery the various combatants had bought — or been given by their friends. Having provided themselves with all these expensive weapons it remained to be seen how they would use them. Would they attack or defend? Would Nasser, having made an offensive move in Strategy, be content with a Tactical defensive? What in short were the Rules by which Generals operated in those days? It was a good question that Alice asked, and one which many a military expert has tried to answer. It would be true to say that every major army has devised, or borrowed, its own list of Principles of War by which the operational planners are guided, and which every officer attempts to remember. For nigh on fifty years the British have clung with commendable tenacity and only minor modifications to a set devised by the late Major-General J. F. C. Fuller, but other nations — notably the Russians — follow a very different list of principles. Currently

---

[17] *Through the Looking-Glass, and What Alice Found There.* By Lewis Carroll, p. 159. Macmillan & Co., 1883.

the British set is:

> Maintenance of the Aim (formerly called the Objective).
> The maintenance of Morale (added after World War II).
> Offensive Action.
> Surprise and Security
> Concentration of Effort and Economy of Force
> (The above two pairs are complementary.)
> Flexibility (formerly called Mobility).
> Co-operation (between Allies, Services and Arms).

Armed with this list the aspiring general should, at any rate in theory, be able to take the field and plan operations that must infallibly bring about the ruin of his adversaries. However, as that remarkable strategist the late Lt. Colonel A. H. Burne pointed out[18] there are other factors (The Strands of War he called them), moral and material, which govern military operations. They are:

> I. The quality and capability of the *commander*.
> II. The quality and capability of the *troops*.
> III. *Morale*.
> IV. *Resources*.

One cannot get to the heart of any campaign without reflecting upon these factors as they affect either side. With regard to the Israeli War of 1967, it must be abundantly clear, that this is a useful classification. In addition Terrain, Weather and Luck, variable factors which are more or less incomputable, demand consideration, for they all have their effect. It may be useful also to take into account the fact that war is carried on on at least four different planes, two strategic

---

[18] *The Art of War on Land*, p. 2. Methuen. London, 1944.

and two tactical. The difference between the two can be clearly, if crudely defined thus: 'Strategy brings the troops to the battlefield: tactics directs their action thereon, Tactics begins where Strategy ends.'[19] This definition is something of an oversimplification. The important thing to realize is that at the highest level strategy is a business for statesmen, even politicians, advised by their military officers, but *not* dictated to. War is a political act: a means of employing Violence to attain the ends of national policy.

In the war under discussion, then, the Grand Strategy was the affair of President Nasser, of King Hussein, of Mr. Eshkol and others, including, of course, General Dayan — but the last-named in his 1967 capacity of minister not his former role of battlefield commander or chief of staff. Strategy at the lower level, the campaign level, must be the affair of the men on the spot, even though they may often find minister or monarch 'breathing down their necks'. In Sinai it fell to General Gavish and General Mortagi to take the command decisions. Their relationship was similar to that of Generals Montgomery and Rommel in the Desert days of the Second World War. However much their political masters may have felt tempted to interfere, the day to day running of the Campaign was in their hands.

Just as Strategy is a matter of two levels so it is with Tactics. Grand Tactics are the broad movements of formations — divisions and brigades in this case — upon the battlefield. On the Sinai front this was the sphere of Generals Tal, Yoffe and Sharon, and of the various Egyptian divisions and brigade commanders whose names — fortunately for their reputations — are so easily forgotten. In the Israel Defence Force, where like Ney or Lasalle in the brave old Napoleonic days, the

---

[19] Burne, *op. cit*, p. 23.

generals like to lead their armies from in front, the distinction between Grand and Minor Tactics tends to become obscured. It is none the less a real one. Minor tactics, the affair of section, platoon and company commanders, are a question of the effective application of firepower, and of swift, sure mobility: in short of Fire and Movement. In attack it is to these junior commanders that falls the vital task of ensuring that their men make the best use of the terrain and of meteorological conditions to give themselves cover, and to get their weapons forward without allowing the momentum of the offensive to ebb away as casualties mount and men tire.

Military historians and commentators make great play with various strategical terms, some simple and some not so easily comprehensible. The main terms dear to their hearts are:

> The Base (of supplies).
> The Lines of Communication (L. of C.).
> A Salient.
> A Re-entrant.
> Forming front to a flank.
> The Strategic Flank.
> An Outflanking movement.
> An Enveloping movement.
> Double Envelopment — 'the pincers movement'.
> To Refuse a Flank.
> Penetration. Single or Double.
> Logistics.
> Interior Lines.
> Exterior Lines.

The armchair strategists of the future will be deeply grateful to the Israelis for giving them so many examples of their Black Art in one short, fell campaign.

As to Supply Bases, that of the Israelis could be said to be their Heartland in the area Haifa-Tel Aviv — very vulnerable be it noted from the air and to a determined thrust from the Jordanian frontier anywhere between Tulkarm and Latrun. The Syrian base area one supposes to be Damascus; the Jordanian is the Amman-Zerqa area; while the Egyptians in Sinai were based West of the Suez Canal. The main Jordanian L. of C. running through Salt, dropping down into the Jordan Valley, crossing the Allenby Bridge and winding up via Jericho to Jerusalem is notoriously vulnerable. The destruction of the bridges and the strafing of the roads from the air would render supply or reinforcement unusually difficult. A similar problem existed on the Northern front in the Nablus-Jenin-Tulkarm sector. In the days when Glubb Pasha commanded the Arab Legion war-wise commanders on the West Bank used to see that their posts were stocked up with sufficient ammunition for at least a fortnight.

The Egyptian L. of C. was perhaps not quite so vulnerable although moving about the Sinai Desert must be rather like trying to operate on the face of the moon. For one thing, in theory there would be powerful air cover. Even so the L. of C. of some formations ran through the Mitla Pass, which one would expect to have seen held in force. The passages of the Suez Canal itself might be vulnerable to air attack. Again it would have been prudent to have kept good stocks of supplies, especially fuel and ammunition, in the forward areas. The question of water supply was bound to be a headache to the Egyptian commanders. When General Sir Archibald Murray moved his 'Egyptian Expeditionary Force' — a largely horse-drawn army be it noted — against Gaza in 1917 he ensured its water supply by a 12-inch pipeline all the way from Qantara to El Arish, thus fulfilling the ancient prophecy that 'when the water of the Nile came to Palestine, Jerusalem would be retaken from the Turks'.[20]

The Jewish part of Jerusalem and Arab-held Latrun were both excellent examples of salients before the Israelis overran the West Bank of Jordan in June 1967. A salient merely means a place where the line bulges outwards into enemy held territory: while a re-entrant is the reverse. A salient in a defensive position will tempt an attacker to try the double envelopment strategy. To form front to a flank means to wheel so that the line is parallel to the L. of C. instead of running away from it. Thus the Israelis in their Central Command around Jerusalem were forming front to a flank facing the Jordanians and protecting their L. of C. to their forces on the Sinai and Syrian fronts. This is a vulnerable position.

In a campaign the attacker often strives to outflank his opponent by a turning movement. The strategic flank is the one whose collapse involves the endangering of the whole position. For General Mortagi in Sinai this was his southern flank, for the north of his line rested on the sea. In the same way during most of the fighting in the Libyan Desert in the Second World War the southern was usually the strategic flank of the British since the Mediterranean, generally controlled by the Royal Navy, covered the northern.

To outflank simply means to extend one's line beyond the enemy's flank. It is an extremely effective movement in tactics, and its effect increases when the enemy depends to an undue extent on fortifications, as did the French in 1940 and indeed the Egyptians and Syrians, and possibly the Jordanians in 1967.

---

[20] See Wavell. *The Palestine Campaigns*, p. 62, fn. 'By a prophet of the Lord,' the prophecy is supposed to have run. General Allenby's name transliterated into Arabic was equivalent to 'Allah en Nebi' — 'the prophet of God'.

Nowadays the mobility of an army depends to a great extent on the standard of education of the rank and file. It is easier to brief educated soldiers, and therefore easier to make them manoeuvre quickly and expertly. Ill-educated troops — like the Turks in Allenby's days — will fight with tenacity in a carefully sited defensive position, but tend to fall to pieces against an army who outmanoeuvres them. To go back a little further in History we find this happening at Castiglione (1796). The Austrians were capable of holding a French frontal attack, but fell into disorder when trying to turn front to a flank. The French, more spirited, more intelligent, and with more initiative, were better able to manoeuvre and had got round their left flank.

For a double envelopment one need only refer to the capture of Jerusalem from the Jordanians. It was a classic example of the pincer's movement, and one which the relatively weakly held Jordanian position in the Old City seemed to render well-nigh inevitable.

As to Penetration, on the Sinai front, the Israelis achieved not merely a double, but a *triple* one.

This was remarkable in itself, but is even more so when one considers the *depth* achieved by the penetration. A simple break-in, followed by a more or less leisurely 'dog-fight' was not good enough for the Israeli generals. They could not afford an eleven day slogging match like Alamein — and not having the Afrika Korps against them did not have to indulge in one. A double penetration can lead to a complex situation, especially if it is not pressed home, because, in theory at any rate, counter-attack by reserves should destroy the spearheads — as happened to the *panzerkeil*[21] at Kursk. But if the Egyptians paid lip service to the Russian defensive tactics of

---

[21] Panzer wedge.

1943 they lacked the fundamental solidity to restore a line once broken.

Logistics is the business of supplying and moving troops, a field in which the Israelis excel, and in which all their opponents are distinctly suspect. One can include the business of mobilization under this heading and no nation had this better organized than Israel.

An army whose Lines of Communication close inward is said to have Interior Lines. The Israelis, simply because they were surrounded, were in this position which meant that troops from their Central Front could be moved without undue difficulty or delay to the Syrian Front. Regarding their enemies as a single whole — which they certainly were not — it could be said that the Arab/Egyptian array was on Exterior Lines, but this would be misleading since their bases were quite separate. Napoleon is quoted as saying 'As for me I am always on interior lines'.[22] It was not strictly true, but at least the remark goes some way to prove the value of interior lines as a strategic concept. In the case of the Israelis prior to the June campaign the interior position was weakened by the extreme narrowness of the 'wasp waist' between Qalqilya and the sea. One former brigadier (British) of the Arab Legion was quick to express to the present writer his forthright opinion on this point. 'Why on earth did Jordan not thrust from Tulkarm instead of wasting their ammo from their funkholes in the Old City?'[23]

There are some who think that fighting has changed completely since the Second World War, and that it follows that the strategic concepts of those days are no longer valid. It is true that changes and improvements in weapons are

---

[22] Burne, *op. cit.*, p. 29.
[23] Letter of 7 June 1967.

modifying tactics all the time. But if the Centurions and T55s of the Sinai campaign are greatly superior to the armour used by O'Connor in 1940 or Montgomery in 1942, the Israelis still use what they are pleased to call their super-Shermans! In fact the swift *blitzkrieg* of June 1967 was very much a campaign of the Second World War. The fate of Graziani's army in 1940 was not so dissimilar to that of Mortagi in 1967. History does not really repeat itself. Rabin's campaign of 1967 which at first seemed to follow the lines of Dayan's of 1956 was really very different. Even so war does not altogether change its patterns, which tend to recur. One must not push historical parallels too far, but it may be said that Israel's position, ironically enough, was not unlike that of the Prussia of King Frederick the Great. He, too, was surrounded by a sea of enemies — Austria, France and Russia. He, too, was willing to risk 'the pre-emptive strike', and having done so struck first at the most formidable of his enemies. Nor was he too nice in his dealings to eschew depriving them — permanently — of a province or two. Here, too, it seems the Israelis are going to behave in a fashion not unlike the Prussia of two centuries ago. It is a curious thought. Israel owes much to the Germans whose pogroms were the hammer that beat their nation into its present shape. It is hardly a service for which the Jews will give thanks to the Teutons. But in the field of strategy they can perhaps afford to acknowledge a debt. Ideas descending from Frederick, via Scharnhorst, Gneisenau and Clausewitz to Manstein, Rommel and Guderian seem to lie at the root of much of the thinking of educated Israeli soldiers like Dayan and Rabin. This is inevitable for it is part of a heritage which is part of the equipment of all professionally alert officers in the Western armies from which the I.D.F. has borrowed much of its technique.

There are those in England who will flatter themselves that the I.D.F. was also strongly influenced by British military thought, and since Dayan, Weizman and Hod, to name but a few, served in the British forces this is not unreasonable. Indeed such an authority as Sir Basil Liddell-Hart has suggested recently[24] that Israeli strategy may owe something to British theory. 'The whole course of the Israeli campaign, a perfect *blitzkrieg*, was of particular interest to me because it was the best demonstration yet of my theory of the strategy of indirect approach, and in its subtler sense of seeking and exploiting "the line of least expectation" — a theory evolved nearly 40 years ago. The Germans, to my chagrin, applied it in 1940, under Guderian's inspiration and influence.'

Sir Basil, the doyen of the British military thinkers of today, goes on to point out that not even Guderian and Rommel grasped 'the subtler side of it so well as the Israeli leaders have done'. Ever since 1948 they have improved upon their strategic methods. 'With each test they have improved — contradicting the experience of history that armies learn only from defeat, not victory.'

The idea that Middle Eastern strategy might owe something to British influence is not altogether immodest. The first *blitzkrieg* of modern times — albeit a horsed one — was after all the great enveloping flanking movement by which in September 1918 Allenby finally cleared the Turks from Palestine and Syria. It will be recalled that breaking through on the Mediterranean coast near Arsuf (where Richard Coeur de Lion had once won a battle) he sent his great mass of 12,000 cavalry on the long ride that took them all the way to Damascus.

---

[24] 'Churchills'-Eye View of a War.' The *Daily Telegraph*, 11 August 1967.

Writing in 1928 the late Field-Marshal Viscount Wavell summed up the Battles of Megiddo in the words of Jeremiah[25]: 'If thou hast run with the footmen, and they have wearied thee, then how canst thou contend with horses?' He wrote at a period when the tank, though already invented, was a ponderous machine as yet unsuited for the *blitzkrieg*. It fell to Guderian and the rest to translate Allenby's concept into terms of armoured warfare using, be it noted, a British invention, the tank.

Roused from the torpor of the 1920s and '30s the British were not so slow to follow the German example and stage a mechanized *blitzkrieg* of their own. Again it was the Middle East that was to witness their triumph.

The Italians had massed 250,000 men in Libya at a time when Wavell had no more than 36,000 in Egypt and something like 85,300 in the entire Middle East. The Italians, of course, had another 350,000 men in Abyssinia. General Wavell, like Robert E. Lee before him and the Israeli generals after him, was not impressed by counting mere numbers — 'cipherin' as Lee called it. The British were instructed to 'make one man appear to be a dozen, make one tank look Eke a squadron, make a raid look like an advance'.[26]

The anglophobia of Graziani, the Italian commander, was tempered by extreme caution and in Abyssinia he had already proved himself 'a veritable snail'[27]. Urged on by Mussolini he crossed the Egyptian frontier in mid-September 1940 and began to build a chain of seven detached forts. These were probably rather less formidable than those since constructed by the Egyptians in Sinai, but in general, though they evidently did

---

[25] xii. 5. See Colonel A. P. Wavell's *The Palestine Campaigns*, p. 203.
[26] Alan Moorehead: *African Trilogy*, pp. 22–3.
[27] Major-General J. F. C. Fuller: *The Second World War*, p. 94.

not realize it, the posture the latter adopted in May 1967 was remarkably like that taken up by Graziani in face of General O'Connor. The Churchills wittily describe Field Marshal Viscount Montgomery's visit to Egypt (3–10 May 1967) as a 'bizarre diversion'. It turned out to be exactly that in the strictly military sense that it deceived. The Field Marshal lectured on desert warfare at the Higher Military Academy. Unfortunately for his audience — though not unnaturally — it was not Graziani's fate that they wished to hear about. As the Churchills put it Montgomery 'described the battle of Alamein and answered a barrage of questions, from the men who were soon to be so disastrously trapped in Sinai. He does not seem to have given them the right answers. Perhaps they did not ask the right questions'.[28] Quite so. It was hardly the Field Marshal's fault if they were not even discussing the right campaign. Had they thought back to Graziani they might have discovered awful warnings more appropriate to their own peculiarly sluggish notions of war.

In 1940, though the R.A.F. more than held its own, the British did not succeed in wresting complete air superiority from their Italian opponents as the Israelis did in 1967. They did, however, have one great advantage — their 50 'I' (Infantry) tanks which, though slow, were much superior to anything Graziani had, and were proof against the 37mm anti-tank gun. The Israelis enjoyed no obvious superiority in quality of armour when they attacked the Egyptians in 1967.

The British began their approach march on the night of 7 December, penetrated a 20-mile gap in the chain of forts which the Italians had left between Nibeiwa and those of Sofafi East and Sofafi West. The forts were taken from the rear, and the main coast road was cut between Buq Buq and

---

[28] Randolph S. and Winston S. Churchill: *The Six Day War*, p. 27.

Sidi Barrani. By 11 December five Italian divisions had been put out of action by a force that never numbered more than two divisions. And so it went on until after 62 days Graziani had lost 10 divisions, 130,000 prisoners, 380 tanks and 845 guns. This exploit cost the British 1,928 casualties. Of course, the range and speed of armour have improved greatly since 1940, but the parallels between the plan of battle hatched in General O'Connor's brain and those of the Israelis of 1967 are striking to say the least. The success of this fine feat of arms, often called 'the Wavell offensive', really depended upon the corps commander. As Field Marshal Lord Harding, then his Chief of Staff,[29] has written 'the grim determination that inspired all our troops stemmed up from his heart; it was his skill in calculating the risks, and his daring in accepting them, that turned what might have been merely a limited success into a victorious campaign with far-reaching effects on the future course of the war'.[30]

So it is not only to the pages of Liddell-Hart or Guderian that we must turn to see what a *blitzkrieg* minded commander, an Allenby, an O'Connor or a Gavish can be expected to make of a campaign in the Middle East. Megiddo 1918 and Libya-Cyrenaica 1940 still have instructive lessons for us.

En passant it may be worth remarking the confusion that existed as to the parts played by Wavell (G.O.C., Middle East), General Sir Henry Maitland-Wilson (G.O.C., Egypt) and O'Connor (corps commander) in 1940. A similar confusion arose in 1967 as to the parts played by Dayan (Minister of Defence), Rabin (Chief of Staff) and Gavish (Southern Command). They all played their parts, but whereas in each

---

[29] Brigadier, General Staff
[30] See the Foreword to Brigadier C. N. Barclay's *Against Great Odds*, p. 5.

case the first two were really concerned with Grand Strategy at the lower level, the corps battle was run, day by day, by O'Connor and Gavish respectively.

If other things were equal the Military Balance in planes, tanks, guns, ships and men would decide the issues of war and the results could be foretold by computer. But since the morale of different troops and the individual skill of their commanders are scarcely susceptible of calculation the Military Balance, though important, is never quite the whole story. The lessons of History and of Strategy must still be analysed and reflected upon if troops are not to become mere pawns, sacrificed by their uncomprehending political masters, as the unfortunate Egyptians were sacrificed by the misguided President Nasser in June 1967.

With some knowledge of the national characteristics of the combatants, of the terrain, and of recent developments in the Art of War, it was not altogether impossible to predict the probabilities of an Arab–Israel War in 1967. It was bound to follow the classic lines of the *blitzkrieg* as evolved between 1918 and 1956, and any observer who put his money on the Egyptians was likely to lose his stake.

CHAPTER V CHRONOLOGY

October 1966: Syrian Prime Minister encourages guerrilla operations against Israel.

4 November 1966: U.A.R. sign defence pact with Syria. Russian technicians speed up installation of SA-2 guided missile sites in Syria.

13 November 1966: Israeli attack on Jordanian village of Samu.

7 April 1967: Clash between Syria and Israel. Six Syrian MiGs shot down. U.A.R. does nothing. U.S.S.R. warns Israel of possible consequences of her 'armed provocation'.

Early May 1967: 'Russian friends' tip off the Egyptian parliamentary delegation to Moscow that Israel is planning to attack Syria.

12 May 1967: Eshkol indicates that Israel is not prepared to tolerate Syrian sabotage raids much longer.

13 May 1967: Syrian Foreign Minister states that Israel is planning aggression.

15 May 1967: Israel Independence Day Parade held in Jerusalem. Egyptian Army begins to concentrate in Sinai Peninsula.

16 May 1967: U.A.R. proclaims a state of emergency for her armed forces.

18 May 1967: Egypt requests the withdrawal of the U.N.E.F. from Egypt.

18 May 1967: Brazilian government signifies willingness to withdraw its 432 men with U.N.E.F. if U Thant agrees to the Egyptian withdrawal request. Hopes tensions will decrease and offers co-operation U.N.O. Brazilian Jews protest against withdrawal of U.N.E.F.

18 May 1967: Egyptian troops re-occupy Sharm-el-Sheikh.

19 May 1967: U Thant announces the withdrawal of U.N.E.F.

22 May 1967: Nasser announces the closing of the Gulf of Aqaba to Israeli shipping and bans the passage of strategic materials to Israel. Withdrawal of U.N.E.F.

23 May 1967: Statement by U.S.S.R. gives verbal support to the Arabs. Gulf of Aqaba closed. Sweden expresses concern at withdrawal of U.N.E.F.

24 May 1967: France suggests consultations between the four great powers.

25 May 1967: Somali Republic promises support for the Arabs. Dutch Foreign Minister criticises U Thant for the speed of U.N.E.F. withdrawal. A Czech statement blames Israeli 'threats of war' for the aggravation of the situation in the Middle East.

27 May 1967: Algeria mobilizes.

29 May 1967: Morocco promises 'effective support' in the event of Israeli aggression.

29 & 30 May 1967: Cuban newspapers (*Granma* and *El Mundo*) blame crisis on U.S. imperialism.

30 May 1967: Reconciliation between King Hussein and Nasser.

31 May 1967: Lima. Israeli Embassy announces that many Peruvian youths have volunteered for the Israeli Army. Iraqi troops reported in Jordan.

1 June 1967: Harsh pronouncement by East Germany aimed at 'imperialists' and Israel.

2 June 1967: President de Gaulle announces that France is in no way committed to either side in the M.E. crisis and is concerned that it should not lead to open war. Egyptians mortar Israeli *kibbutzim* and set wheatfields on fire. Egyptian and Syrian envoys visit Algiers seeking support. Norwegian

Foreign Ministry statement favours 'free and innocent passage' of the Straits of Tiran for the ships of any country. Belgian government, disturbed by M.E. crisis, announces that it will participate in all initiatives to reduce tension.

4 June 1967: Two Egyptian 'commando' battalions and an Iraqi division arrive in Jordan.

5 June 1967: The campaign begins.

CHAPTER V: THE MAY CRISIS

And there was a great cry of the people and of their wives against their brethren the Jews.

Nehemiah, 5:1.

The Israeli Campaign of June 1967 was the direct result of an exercise in brinkmanship. It is not unreasonable to assume that the Soviet Union had no special object in view when the crisis built up in May 1967. Russia was working within the general aims of her foreign policy, and it is probably not being too cynical to describe these as, firstly the embarrassment of the West, more particularly the Western Superpower; secondly the extension of Russian influence and thirdly the extension of Communist influence. Supposing that the Russians were aware that the U.S.A. was in fact stronger than the U.S.S.R. it is not unreasonable to assume that the Kremlin would be happy to see American resources extended. A time when a vast army was already deployed in Vietnam was clearly an appropriate moment for a crisis elsewhere. The Middle East was not an unattractive theatre for such an operation.

There was powerful support for Israel in the U.S.A., and for that reason Mr. Lyndon B. Johnson's government could scarcely allow Israel to go under. There are some 5,725,000 Jews in the U.S.A. — well over twice the number in Israel — and though only 3 per cent of the total population they are, from a political point of view, strongly posted:

New York City: 1,835,000
Adjoining boroughs: 545,000

Los Angeles: 490,000
Philadelphia: 330,000
Chicago: 285,000
Boston: 169,000

Well-educated, public-spirited and strategically deployed it was not an ethnic group which any American administration — especially one with an election a year ahead — could lightly affront.

Mounting tension on the Arab-Israeli front might well compel Western powers to come out strongly in favour of Israel. This would be the time for discreet support of the Arabs. Normal propaganda, Arab rather than Russian, could be trusted to show the Egyptians and the Syrians who were their friends and who their foes. All this would come far short of war, although it might leave the Arabs some trophy of diplomatic victory, such as the closing of the Gulf of Aqaba.

There was, it is true, some risk of a local, limited war, but with the Egyptian and Syrian forces fully equipped with Russian weapons there was little risk of a repetition of 1956. Even if the Arabs were not yet capable of carrying out an effective offensive, they ought to be able to hold out on the defensive for some weeks. After all they had been thoroughly indoctrinated in Soviet defensive tactics, with line after line of fortified positions supported by mobile, armoured, counter-attack forces and artillery. If there was fighting, and if it went wrong, it would probably end in a deadlock. A talking match would ensue in the United Nations, and the Russians would have very considerable opportunities for propaganda. Chinese criticism would be countered; much play could be made with demands for American concessions in Vietnam — as if the U.S.S.R. should wish to see the U.S.A. freed from that trap!

And in the meanwhile the West's oil supplies would have been jeopardized.

Russia worked diligently for reconciliation between the 'progressive' Arab States — the U.A.R., Syria, Iraq and Algeria. Syrian Ba'athists buried the hatchet with Nasser.

Beyond question Syria rather than the other Arab powers made the running in the months leading up to the June campaign. The Ba'ath[31] government, lacking broad-based popular support, was in the classic posture of depending on a foreign adventure to rally public opinion at home. The Palestine Problem, with the very genuine question of the refugees unsettled, was a great stand-by. Devotion to this Holy War (*Jihad*) was proof that the Syrians were better Arabs than the Egyptians. The Ba'athist brand of socialism, by attracting Soviet support, gave the regime a measure of respectability, which was enhanced by loud and ceaseless propaganda and constant terrorist raids by the Fa'tah into Israel.

When on 4 November 1966 all this activity led to a defence pact between Syria and the U.A.R. there was considerable surprise in Western circles, for it was obvious that the Syrian Ba'athists were really bitterly opposed to Nasser. Nevertheless the alliance seemed to be fairly effective, not to say formidable, and when on 13 November the Israelis, their patience exhausted by countless raids, struck back, it was not at Syria but at Jordan. The Israelis were well aware that the Fa'tah raids, even if they came across the frontiers of Lebanon or Jordan, were Syrian-inspired and one was at a loss to explain

---

[31] The Ba'ath party stands for freedom, Marxist socialism and Pan-Arab unity of a nationalistic type reminiscent of Hitler's Germany. Nasser is a rival simply because he is not a Ba'athist. The Ba'ath is not Communist.

this event. Were they afraid to tackle the Syrian 'Maginot Line' on the rugged plateau west of Qnaitra? Did they *want* to thrust Jordan into the arms of Egypt?

The Samu incident was a serious one, on a scale similar to the Qalqilya raid that heralded the Sinai campaign of 1956.[32] The U.N. condemned Israel for this operation in which there were 18 killed and 134 wounded, and 127 buildings destroyed. The Jordanian Air Force, fighting against odds, lost a Hunter shot down.

There was to be one more 'headline' incident before the serious fighting started. That was when on 7 April 1967, as a result of Syrian interference with cultivation near the frontier, the Israeli Air Force came out and six Syrian MiGs were shot down. The significance of this episode was that the U.A.R. did exactly nothing about it.

It was early in May that 'Russian friends' intimated to an Egyptian Parliamentary delegation visiting Moscow that the Israelis were planning to attack Syria.

To Nasser this tip must have seemed confirmed when, on 12 May, Levi Eshkol, Prime Minister of Israel, let it be known that Syrian sabotage operations could not be borne much longer: 'In view of the 14 incidents in the past month alone, we may have to adopt measures no less drastic than those of April 7.'

On 15 May Israel held her Independence Day Parade in Jerusalem. Although this had been done before when Ben Gurion was Prime Minister it was not without danger, for the armistice agreement of 1949 restricted both Israeli and Jordanian forces in the sector to two battalions, while aircraft and armour were altogether excluded. The representatives of the Great Powers declined invitations. The parade did not in

---

[32] See General Moshe Dayan's *Diary of the Sinai Campaign* for an account of this episode.

fact exceed the permitted strength, but the Arabs put a sinister construction on this. Egyptian intelligence is thought to have explained the absence of modern heavy weapons in the march past at Jerusalem by telling the Syrians that 14 Israeli brigades had been concentrated within a few miles of their border. Whether this information was correct or not is still uncertain, but the Syrian Foreign Minister had already (13 May) stated that Israel was planning aggression. The aim, it seems, was the liquidation of the revolutionary regime in Syria, which Rabin had hinted at as early as 10 May.

The situation was fraught with difficulty for Nasser. He had failed the Syrians on 7 April. His leadership of the Arab World would be seriously questioned if he should do nothing yet again. On 16 May a state of emergency for the U.A.R. armed forces was proclaimed, and on 18 May Egypt requested the withdrawal of U.N.E.F.

There can be little doubt that Nasser expected that U Thant would agree to his request. But no Arab would expect acquiescence except as a consequence of fairly prolonged bargaining — not less than a fortnight. U.N.E.F. included Yugoslav and Indian troops, as well as Brazilians. It may be that U Thant was under pressure from some of their governments to comply with Nasser's request. Though some condemned his precipitation, there can be little question that he was bound to accede, though not necessarily without argument. In U Thant's favour it can be urged that he did no more than accede to a *fait accompli*.

Nasser, thrown like a man whose Judo opponent suddenly falls over backwards, now felt compelled to pour troops into Sinai. With 100,000 men and some 900 tanks at his command he felt strong enough to reoccupy Sharm-el-Sheikh, and on 22 May he announced the closing of the Gulf of Aqaba to Israeli shipping. The passage of strategic materials to Eilat was banned.

Many and varied were the responses that this state of affairs evoked. If the U.S.A., Great Britain and France wished to avoid conflict the same can perhaps be said of the Israeli government also. Eshkol and his Foreign Minister, Abba Eban, were, after all, moderates, and it is suspected that the former favoured negotiation rather than a resort to arms. But the mood of the country was less mild. The *Sabra* (cactus)[33] Cult is strong in Israel. It is a rugged, self-confident creed, that imbues the army, and in Israel the army sets the pace. One tenet of this creed is that the Israelis do not mean to follow the European Jews of a generation ago — *The Sapōn* — into the gas-chambers, or something equally unattractive. Public opinion compelled Eshkol to turn to Rafi, Ben Gurion's splinter group, and bring in the victor of Sinai, General Moshe Dayan. The former terrorist Menachim Begin was also brought into the cabinet. Dayan follows a much tougher line than Eshkol. Given the distinctly cautious attitude of the Western Powers it was obvious that once Dayan was Minister of Defence, Israel would 'go it alone'.

The crisis was having repercussions, some predictable, some not.

The Scandinavian powers favoured Israel. On 23 May the Swedish Foreign Minister expressed concern at the withdrawal of U.N.E.F., foreseeing the danger of war if Nasser should prevent Israeli shipping passing through the Straits of Tiran. Danish public opinion supported Israel almost unanimously, and in the Security Council Denmark and Canada were joint sponsors of a resolution calling for a ceasefire. On 2 June Norway stated that the Straits must be considered international

---

[33] Israelis born in Israel are called *Sabra*.

and that no state bordering on those waters had the right to prevent the 'free and innocent passage' of the ships of any country.

Holland criticised the speed of U Thant's withdrawal of U.N.E.F. (25 May).

The French government approached the crisis with the greatest caution, its representatives everywhere counselling calm and moderation. On 24 May consultations between the four great powers were suggested, not that France dissociated herself from the efforts of the United Nations. According to *Le Monde* (26 May) the French government preferred 'discreet diplomacy' to a summit meeting.

Israel was disappointed at what seemed to her a lukewarm attitude. But the ally of 1956 had meanwhile improved her image in the Arab world by terminating the bloody war in Algeria. It was left to Monsieur Lecanuet, president of the Democratic Centre Party, to express solidarity with Israel and to deplore the government's failure to side with her (*Le Monde*, 27 May).

On 2 June President de Gaulle is alleged to have told a Council of Ministers that France was in no way committed to either side of the states involved in the Middle East crisis and was chiefly concerned that it should not lead to open war. The state which should first resort to arms would have neither the support nor the approval of France.

The attitude of Great Britain, Israel's other ally of 1956, was scarcely more positive. Concerned, not unnaturally, for her oil supplies, she was determined to work within the framework of U.N.O., though she did declare strongly in favour of freedom of navigation in the Gulf of Aqaba.

Italy also pursued a moderate line based on 'respect for the independence and autonomy of all peoples in the Middle East'.

On 27 May Algeria mobilized and on 2 June Zakaria Mohieddin (U.A.R.) and Ibrahim Murkos (Syria) arrived in Algiers, seeking support. President Boumédiène delivered himself of the opinion (4 June) that 'the challenge facing the Arab World was not a matter of race or religion, but the existence of Israel as a base of British and American imperialism', while his chief of staff opined that 'there will be war'. At that range he could risk it. The same day the Somali Premier declared his full support for Arab states and offered 'whatever assistance we can provide'. But in his case desire bade fair to outrun performance.

Morocco also promised (29 May) that in the event of Israeli aggression it would provide 'effective support'. The news that King Hussein had been reconciled to Nasser was received with acclamation.

In these tense weeks nobody was faced with more perplexing decisions than King Hussein of Jordan. To listen to Cairo or Damascus radio one would suppose that the Hashemite King was a Western puppet, a reactionary working hand in glove with Israel, and the numerous Palestinian refugees in his country lent willing ears to nonsense of this sort. With the *Jihad* gathering momentum daily he had no alternative but to join the alliance dedicated to win back the lost homes of so many of his subjects. Even so his reconciliation with Nasser (30 May) came as something of a surprise. Although an Egyptian lieutenant-general, Abdul Mu'nim Riad, was put in command of the Jordan Arab Army and Egyptian commandos were sent to operate from Jordan, the Jordanian-U.A.R. Treaty came too late to ensure proper coordination of the Arab war effort. The arrival of Iraqi troops may have influenced the Israeli decision to strike.[34]

---

[34] Exactly when they arrived is not quite clear. The Churchills give

On Friday 2 June General Moshe Dayan took over the direction of the Israel Defence Forces. Israel had now been mobilized for about a fortnight. It did not take a major prophet to foresee that with Dayan back a solution to the crisis would not be deferred many days. As soon as it was clear that the Western Powers were not in fact going to do anything about ensuring freedom of navigation to Eilat, it was obvious that Israel must strike. Nor, according to Dayan, did she in fact want British and American boys to die in her cause. Supremely self-confident, the I.D.F., brought to a razor sharpness by the two weeks' training since mobilization, would cut its own Gordian knots.

When on 5 June an expectant world heard that the explosion had come it was almost a relief. Brinkmanship had gone too far. The superpowers had proved incapable of controlling either Syria or Israel. The puppets preferred to move their own limbs. It was not to be expected that Russia could predict how quickly U.N.E.F. would be withdrawn. It remained to be seen whether the Arabs, with all their new weaponry, and with plenty of time to 'get set', would be able to stand up to the army which, in the words of one of its own generals, Sharon, 'looked like a mob'. A British officer, who visited the I.D.F. in August 1966, commented: 'If I sensed a weakness in battle readiness then it lies in a tendency to train for the 1956 Sinai campaign in 1966…'

1956 was just a dress rehearsal!

---

three different dates: 24 May (p. 126), 31 May (p. 52 & p. 77) and 4 June (p. 70).

CHAPTER VI CHRONOLOGY

SEA

19 May 1967: Israeli Navy begins mobilization.

5 June, Night, 1967: Israeli attacks on Port Said and Alexandria.

6 June 1967: Egyptian Navy withdrawn from Port Said.

6 June, Night, 1967: Three Egyptian submarines attacked off Haifa and Ashdod.

AIR

5 June, 0745, 1967: First Israeli airstrike on Egyptian airfields.

5 June, 1035, 1967: Egyptian Air Force now virtually destroyed.

5 June, c. 1200, 1967: Syrian raid on oil refinery at Haifa. Jordanians attack Kfar Sirkin. Israelis attack Damascus air base.

5 June, c. 1215, 1967: Jordan. Israelis attack Amman and Mafraq airfields, and Ajlun radar stations.

5 June, Afternoon, 1967: Israeli attacks on 23 Egyptian radar stations.

6 June, Morning, 1967: Iraqi Air Force attacks Netanya. Israelis attack H.3.

8 June 1967: U.S.S. *Liberty* attacked off El Arish.

CHAPTER VI: SEA AND AIR

'We had to batter them before they could batter us.'
Israeli Naval Officer.

The naval side of the 1967 fighting, creditable though it was to General Erell and the Israeli Navy need not detain us long. For this there are two very good reasons. The first is that very little information has emerged on the subject. The second is that the Egyptian navy was prudent to a degree almost incredible even to those with some knowledge of their ways.

On the night of 5 June the Israelis fought one of the most economical battles in Naval History. There was no moon and it was extremely dark. Two forces, carrying men of the frogman-commando trained and led by Yochai Bin-Nun, who at 43 was already a *retired* Commander-in-Chief of the Israeli Navy, approached Alexandria and Port Said.

Off the entrance to Alexandria harbour a submarine — the only operational one the Israelis had — launched its frogmen who penetrated the harbour. None returned, though six were afterwards reported captured. It is believed that they damaged or destroyed two Egyptian submarines and two of the *Osa* missile-carriers.[35]

At Port Said there was a clash involving an Israeli destroyer which, with some MTBs, was taking the frogmen to their target. Two *Osas* were routed by 20mm cannon fire. Here the frogmen found no warships, and refrained from blowing up two oil tankers for fear of causing civilian casualties. There

---

[35] Churchill, p. 95.

probably really were *Osa* and *Komar* missile-carriers at Port Said, for the distance thence to Tel Aviv is only 200 miles, whereas Alexandria to which the Egyptian Navy is reported to have withdrawn next day[36] is 350 miles. The Israeli advance in Sinai, swift though it was, hardly warranted so swift a withdrawal.

On the night of 6 June three separate Egyptian submarines were detected off the Israeli coast, due to using their periscopes too much, and depth charged, one at least being damaged.

The Israelis endeavoured by bluff to persuade the Egyptians that they had a fair-sized amphibious lift at Eilat. In fact they seem to have had three MTBs and four landing craft. This seems to have been successful in making the Egyptians think that as in 1956 they might make a seaborne landing at Sharm-el-Sheikh. At any rate it is estimated that on 5 June 30 per cent of the Egyptian Navy was in the Red Sea[37]. An Egyptian flotilla steamed half-way up the Gulf of Aqaba on the night of 6 June, but turned back without risking contact.

One result of Nasser's reaction to his defeat has received little comment. The substantial squadron of the Egyptian Navy that was in the Red Sea before the campaign was cut off from its bases, Port Said and Alexandria, when the Suez Canal was blocked. These ships are now reported to be based on Hodeida in the Yemen.

Israeli losses seem to have been confined to their frogmen. It is calculated that the Egyptians lost three submarines, three *Osa* and three *Komar* patrol boats[38]. This is a moderate computation for in an interesting article in the *Sunday Times*[39] David Leitch

---

[36] Churchill, p. 95.
[37] Churchill, p. 98.
[38] Figures released by The Institute for Strategic Studies.

reported that on the first night of the war the Israeli Navy crippled all but two of the eleven Egyptian submarines, and, it would seem, most of their missile-carrying patrol-boats.

It may be noted that Israel, with notable forbearance, refrained from making any attack on the Jordanian port of Aqaba, which lies opposite Eilat and is the base for a few patrol craft.

The success of the Israeli Navy will not blind the government of the country to its extreme and dangerous weakness. It is understandable under the circumstances that the defence budget should go to the air force and the army, but Russian built patrol craft carrying missiles with 1,000lb warheads and a range of 35 miles cannot be taken lightly. It is not unreasonable to predict that Israel will feel compelled to build up her navy before the next bout with Egypt, and it may be that some of the maritime powers whose interests have been flouted by Nasser's closure of the Suez Canal, may feel disposed to help her, the more so since a Russian naval squadron in the Egyptian Mediterranean ports may not be altogether welcome to the United States.

'We squeezed the best out of ourselves and the hell out of the enemy.'
Ezer Weizman[40]

In a limited war situation the classic method of conducting air operations is in three phases.

Phase One. Destruction of the enemy's air potential — preferably on the ground.

---

[39] 25 June, 1967.
[40] Telegram to the Author. 27 June 1967.

Phase Two. Interdiction and destruction of the enemy's power to supply his armies.

Phase Three. Offensive air support of the ground forces.

All these phases can be clearly detected in the Israeli air strategy.

Phase One in the Sinai campaign lasted from 0745 to 1035 on 5 June. During this time it is estimated that 300 out of some 340 serviceable Egyptian combat aircraft, including all their TU-16 bombers, were destroyed.

Altogether 19 Egyptian airfields were attacked on 5 June, ten[41] in the first strike at 0745, and nine later[42]. At all, except El Arish, which the Israelis wanted to use themselves, the runways were put out of action.

The Jordanian and Syrian Air Forces showed no signs of life until about noon, by which time, of course, the back of their Egyptian ally's Air Force was already broken. General Mordechai Hod, the commander of the Israeli Air Force, commented: 'We were able to deal with Syria and Jordan in twenty-five minutes.'

On the afternoon of 8 June an Israeli dive-bomber and three MTBs attacked the U.S.S. *Liberty* off El Arish causing much damage besides killing 34 and wounding 75 of the crew. The U.S.A. has accepted Israel's explanation that this was a mistake, though one is not quite clear why an American Electronic Intelligence vessel should be mistaken for an Egyptian destroyer. The United States Defence Department issued a statement that the vessel's object was 'to assure communications between United States Government posts in

---

[41] El Arish, Gebel Libni, Bit Gifgafa, Bir Thamada, Abu Sueir, Kabrit, Inchas, Cairo West, Beni Sueif and Fayid.

[42] Mansura, Helwan, El Minya, Almaza, Luxor, Deversoir, Hurghada, Ras Banas and Cairo International.

the Middle East and to assist in relaying information concerning the evacuation of American citizens from the countries of the Middle East'. A military commentator may be forgiven for suggesting that with the Russian warships monitoring wireless traffic, and the British listening in from Mount Troodos in Cyprus, it was at least possible that the *Liberty* was similarly employed. At a time when the singularly futile problem 'Who fired first?' was exercising so many minds, it may be supposed that the Israelis resented such 'snooping'.

The success of Phase One of the Israeli Plan was remarkable. President Nasser found it incredible and convinced himself — and King Hussein[43] — that it was impossible without the participation of the Americans and the British[44]. This story seems to have convinced their Arab but not their Russian friends. Was Nasser lying or was he simply incredulous? For once it seems possible to give him the benefit of the doubt. He had not had the advantage of an interview with General Ezer Weizman, the man who built the modern Israeli Air Force. He had not seen the excellent air cover which the Israelis had of every Egyptian installation along the Canal Zone.

In October 1966 the author discussed with General Weizman the possible outcome of another campaign against Egypt, and discovered to his surprise that — so far as was known — neither by accident nor design had a single Egyptian plane strayed over the Israeli border since 1956. Yet in the

---

[43] The author was present at a Press conference at the Jordan Embassy in London after the war when King Hussein stated that he no longer believed this story. In view of French and British bombing of Egypt in 1956 he had not thought it incredible.

[44] On 8 June the Israelis released a monitored and somewhat garbled telephone conversation in which Nasser and King Hussein apparently agreed to put out this story. This conversation is said to have taken place at 4.50 on 6 June.

photos of Egyptian SA-2 sites one could count the very missiles. 'We will hack them out of the sky', was the general's comment. It was not difficult to believe of people so dedicated and efficient, who had every last detail worked out. In the words of General Hod: 'We lived with the plan, we slept on the plan, we are the plan. Constantly we perfected it.'

Although this famous plan followed classic lines it had a number of interesting features, and its calculations were nicely made with a fine psychological judgment.

Zero Hour (0845 Egyptian Time) was chosen for various reasons. The mist over the target area would be clear, the dawn 'stand-to' would be over, but, a delightful touch, Egyptian commanders, due to arrive at their offices at 0900, would be late for the battle![45]

The initial Israeli airstrikes were made by flying very low, perhaps as low as 30 feet, in order to get under the radar. In some cases surprise was possible by flying in from the Mediterranean and not directly across the Sinai Desert.

The magazine *Flight International* (22 June 1967) published an interesting article by Robert R. Rodwell, *The Bomb That Won the War*, describing the missile evolved by the Israelis in order to ground the Egyptian Air Force by potholing the runways. *The New Scientist* (28 June 1967) followed this up with a description of the so-called 'dibber' bomb. Armed with this the strike aircraft could make their run in at a height of only 200 feet, discharging their missiles at a speed of 600 m.p.h. 'The bomb is decelerated as it leaves the aeroplane by four forward-firing explosive charges set between its fins. When its nose is thus turned down, a booster in the rear supplements the force of gravity to improve its penetration.'

---

[45] Cf. Churchill, p. 79.

This device overcomes the tendency for a fast-moving bomb to skip or slide. There is no longer any risk that a pilot will blow himself up with his own bomb. The 'dibber' bomb is said to be a 500-pounder, 8 feet long and 1 foot in diameter. There is no reason to doubt that the Israelis invented it themselves, for they certainly believe in keeping abreast of technological advances. In order to discourage repairs some bombs were fitted with time fuses.

Deception was another feature of the plan, Israeli activity over the Gulf of Aqaba, in the days previous to the war, induced the Egyptians to send 20 MiGs from Cairo or the Canal Zone to Hurghada and two destroyers from the Mediterranean to the Red Sea.[46]

The organization of the Israeli aircraft deserves comment. Some pilots are said to have made eight sorties a day. An Egyptian would think he had done well if he had done two. The claim that the Israeli Air Force flew more than 1,000 sorties on 5 and 6 June is, therefore, a modest one. Owing to the efficiency of the ground staff it was just possible for an Israeli pilot to make his second attack within an hour of his first! It was General Hod's proud claim that 'At 0745 Monday morning [5 June] the serviceability of our combat aircraft was better than 99 per cent and we maintained that level of serviceability throughout the week of the war.' Half-measures were useless to the Israelis, a point that is illustrated by the fact that no more than twelve planes were left to guard their home bases. Concentration of Force is no bad Principle of War, but it is seldom exemplified with such ruthless clarity. Nasser was no more than human if he judged the Israeli pilots by the standards of his own. He may be forgiven if he just did not

---

[46] Churchill pp. 80 and 98.

believe that the Israelis could have done all the damage on their own. For indeed they had performed miracles.

Egyptian anti-aircraft fire was probably less effective than the Israelis expected. Observers everywhere were anxious to see how the Russian SA-2 (surface-to-air) missile would perform. Several were fired, but no hits were scored, presumably because the Israeli pilots usually flew too low for them to be effective. 'They gain speed very slowly and for this reason are useless below 4,000ft. above ground level.'[47] It may be that the Churchills go too far in writing of its 'uselessness', but certainly on its Sinai showing the SA-2 can afford little comfort to its Soviet manufacturers.

By the end of the second day's fighting the Arab and Egyptian Air Forces had lost some 416 aircraft, including helicopters. The Egyptians had lost all their big bombers; the Jordanians had lost their whole Air Force. Even Lebanon had managed to lose a Hunter though fortunately for her Israel was good enough not to construe this as meaning that the two countries were at war. The Egyptians are thought to have lost about 100 pilots, caught taxiing on their runways for the most part. In addition to the loss of SA-2 sites, 23 radar stations were destroyed.

The Israelis lost 26 aircraft in the first two days, of which six were *Magisters*. Of the pilots five escaped, four more were exchanged later by the Jordanians and Iraqis. Two are in Egyptian hands. The chances of this war are more than ordinarily random. Another pilot was hacked to pieces by Egyptian villagers, while two are said to have been crucified by the Syrians.

---

[47] Churchill, p. 84.

It is not easy to be certain of the strength of the opposing air forces but the figures below may serve as a guide as to losses.[48]

BALANCE OF THE AIR FORCES
Israel: 4 June: 320, 31 July: 230
Egypt: 4 June: 450[49], 31 July: 225
Syria: 4 June: 106, 31 July: 25
Jordan: 4 June: 28, 31 July: 0
Iraq: 4 June: 170–200, 31 July: 230
Lebanon: 4 June: 18, 31 July: 18[50]

It is naturally impossible to obtain absolutely satisfactory figures. The rise in the Iraqi Air Force is largely accounted for by the fact that by the end of July she had 6 TU-16 medium jet bombers and 50 MiG-21 interceptors that the Institute did not show in its 4 June list. The heavy drop in Israeli aircraft is accounted for by the 48 *Skyhawk* light bombers, thought possibly non-operational on 4 June, being omitted from the July list.

The most significant point about the Israeli air losses is General Hod's claim that: 'In actual dog-fights between aircraft the score was 50-nil. We shot down 50 MiGs in aerial combat without losing one single one of our aircraft.' Such losses as were sustained were due to ground fire or to being 'jumped' while making a ground attack. It is evident that the Egyptian pilots are not in the same league as the Israelis. It follows that if he wishes to embark on a fourth campaign, always supposing Russia to be willing to re-equip him, President Nasser may well be compelled to consider employing 'volunteer' pilots. Let us

---

[48] These figures kindly supplied by *The Institute for Strategic Studies* are those released to the Press on 4 June 1967, and the estimated strength at 31 July.
[49] Some would be in the Yemen and not all would be serviceable.
[50] The implication is that Lebanon has replaced her lost *Hunter*.

hope that such a loss of face will be unacceptable to the Egyptians.

The rout of the Egyptian Air Force must not blind us to the fact that they had laid plans aimed to produce a very different result. Desire outran performance, but it was Egyptian execution, rather than Egyptian staff work that was at fault.

On 17 May Lt.-General Jallal Ibrahim Zaid, Chief of Staff, Eastern Air Command issued Battle Order 1/67 to O.C. 2 Air Brigade.[51]

> 18 Squadron from 259 Air Base with a strength of one flight, will cover the area of aerial umbrella No. 2 (30 kms. east of El Arish) at an altitude of 3000 m., from H. Hour plus 10 to H Hour plus 60, for a 50 minute period.
>
> ASSIGNMENT: protection of our aircraft returning and landing at 259 and 248 air bases.
>
> Control point: Bir Al Abid. Alternative: El Arish.
>
> The remainder of the squadron will maintain 1, 2 state of readiness.

Battle Order 2/67 of 19 May details targets. It is signed by the GOC Eastern Air Region, Lt.-General Abdal Hamid Abd Al Salim Daghidi. The essentials of this TOP SECRET order are:

> 1. 2 Air Brigade
>   a. Squadrons 18 (MiG-17F), and 31 (MiG-17F) to be stationed at 259 air base, under command of 2 Air Brigade.
>   b. 16 Squadron (MiG-17F) of 2 Air Brigade to destroy enemy aircraft at AQIR airbase … at H-hour.

---

[51] I wish to express my thanks to my friend Arie Hashavia who sent me a copy of 'Egyptian Attack Orders against Israel', published in June 1967. This brochure reproduces translations of orders captured at El Arish and El-Ser airfields in the Sinai Peninsula.

c. 31 Squadron (MiG-17F) to destroy HAWK missile placements located in the environs and south of TEL AVIV, at H-Hour.

2. 12 Air Brigade

a. 24 squadron (MiG-15) and 25 squadron (MiG-17F) under command of 12 Air Brigade. 24 squadron (MiG-15) to be located at 248 airbase with the Brigade H.Q.

b. 24 Squadron of 2 Air Brigade from 248 airbase to destroy three radar installations at the following enemy bases (one flight to each target), at H-Hour: radar station at HATZERIM, radar station at BEER MENUHA…, G.H.Q. and Operations Room at Mt. ARIHA…

3. 15 Air Brigade

20 Squadron (MiG-19) of 15 Air Brigade from 224 airbase, to destroy enemy aircraft at QASTINA airfield at H-Hour.

4. 61 Air Brigade

a. 61 Air Brigade, located at 229 airbase, to destroy and neutralize enemy aircraft at BEER SHEBA (HATZERIM) airfield … with a force of 9 aircraft, at H-Hour plus 3.

b. 61 Air Brigade to be prepared to destroy and neutralize BEER MENUHA airfield in southern Negev, with a force of 6 aircraft, at H-Hour.

c. 61 Air Brigade with a force of 6 aircraft to be prepared to destroy the H.Q. at ARIHA … at H-Hour plus 3.

5. 25 squadron (MiG-17F) to be located at 228 airbase.

6. 1 Air Brigade to prepare to participate in action to gain air superiority after the first concentrated bombing, in accordance with orders to be received at the time.

7. 65 Air Brigade, to prepare to attack HATZERIM airfield, near BEER SHEBA … with a force of 4 TU-6 aircraft, at H-Hour.

8. All units participating in the action are to be prepared to deliver a second concentrated blow on the target, 175 minutes after the first concentrated attack. Unit assignments and targets to be determined in accordance with results of aerial observation following the first concentrated attack.

9. All air units are to be prepared to execute four concentrated attacks per day, and a bomber night sortie on the first day of air superiority, at a rate of five sorties of fighter-bombers during the day and three sorties of bombers a day.
10. Air units are to be prepared during the time lapses between concentrated attacks to carry out successive air attacks at flight strength. Each unit is to be given its targets in turn, to prevent the enemy from reconsolidating his air forces.
11. Units on assignments are to maintain an altitude of less than 200m. above ground level, during flight to targets.
12. Air units to assure that 30% of the cannon ammunition remains in reserve for self-defence purposes while returning to base.
13. Air units are to remain over the targets as brief a period as possible.

This was followed up on 21 May by an Annex:

During the operations the Air Formations and Units in the Eastern Air Command will act as follows:
1. 2 Air Brigade
a. Squadron 18 MIG 17-F at Air Base 259 will destroy Aqir Air Base at H-Hour…
b. Squadron 25 MIG 17-F at Air Base 259 will destroy the enemy's missile bases around and south of Tel-Aviv at H-Hour plus 1 minute.
c. Squadron 24 MIG 15 based at Air Base 248 will destroy the enemy's radar installations in the following areas at H-Hour plus 3 minutes:
1. Hatzerim radar station…
2. Beer Menuha Radar station
3. Ariha Command Headquarters…
2. 15 Air Brigade
Squadron 20 MIG 19 based at air base 244 will destroy Kastina Air Field (Kfar-Sirkin …) at H-Hour.

3. 61 Air Brigade

Air Brigade No. 61 will be on standby at air base 229 for the following:
- a. To strike Hatzerim Air Field ... at H-Hour, with its 9 aircraft.
- b. To strike Beer Menuha Air Field in the Southern Negev ... at H-Hour, with 6 of its aircraft.
- c. To strike Ariha Command Headquarters... with 3 of its aircraft.
- d. Squadron No. 31 MIG 17 based at Air Base No. 286 will be ready to supply air support and air defence for the forces situated at Sharm El Sheikh.

Battle Order No. 3/67 of 18 May detailed the air support allocated for the exploitation of the ground offensive intended to cut off the southern Negev and the conquest of Eilat. Here is part of it:

2.
- a. 27 fighter-bombardment squadron sorties from 2 and 12 Air Brigades stationed at 2 bases, Nos. 248 and 249.
- b. 3 light bomber squadron sorties by Air Brigade 61 from Base No. 229.
- — and a sortie of heavy bombing squadron from the reserves of the Air Force O.C. and Air Defence, for the benefit of the operation. Decided upon at the Conference of the Air Force O.C. and Air Defence.

3. *Maximum Daily Effort*

— 9 fighter-bombardment squadron sorties and a light bomber squadron sortie.

4. The sorties will be ordered directly through the Air Support Units at the air bases. Ops. Room No. 50 will monitor the same frequency.

Bombing directions will be effected by the Air Support Liaison officers from forward control points...

7. Air forces will bomb Eilat airfield, the radio station, and the oil storage areas in an effort designated for that purpose by the Air Forces O.C.

This was elaborated in further orders — Battle Order 6/67 of 26 May, signed by Lt.-Colonel Mamdukh Ahmed Taliba, O.C. 2 Air Brigade, concluded with this paragraph:

7. *Duration of State of Readiness*
State of Readiness will commence at dawn of 26.5.1967.
H-Hour will be determined by O.C. air forces and Air Defence.

Amendations to the original plan were issued on 27/5/67. It would be tedious to detail the whole of these orders, but there is ample evidence that the possibility of an offensive on or after 26 May was very much on the cards. On the ground General Mortagi — like Graziani in 1940 — was content to adopt a defensive posture. His Air Force colleagues, placid though they had been since 1956, were certainly going through the motions of planning an offensive.

APPENDIX
The Nasser–King Hussein Telephone Conversation

Nasser: How are you? The brother wants to know if the fighting is going on all along the front.
Will His Majesty make an announcement on the participation of Americans and British?
Hussein: (Answer not clear.)
Nasser: Hello, will we say the U.S. and England or just the U.S.?
Hussein: The U.S. and England.
Nasser: Does Britain have aircraft carriers?
Hussein: (Answer not clear.)
Nasser: Good. King Hussein will make an announcement and I

will make an announcement.

We are fighting with all our strength and we have battles going on on every front all night and if we had any trouble in the fighting it does not matter, we will overcome despite this. God is with us. Will His Majesty make an announcement on the participation of the Americans and the British?

Hussein: (Answer not clear.)

Nasser: By God, I say that I will make an announcement and you will make an announcement and we will see to it that the Syrians will make an announcement that American and British airplanes are taking part against us from aircraft carriers. We will issue an announcement. We will stress the matter and we will drive the point home.

Hussein: Good. All right.

Nasser: A thousand thanks. Do not give up. We are with you with all our heart and we are flying our planes over Israel today, our planes are striking at Israel's airfields since morning.

CHAPTER VII CHRONOLOGY

5 June 1967: Israeli advance begins. Kuntilla taken.

6 June 1967: Capture of El Arish, Abu Agheila stormed, Gaza, and Ras en Naqb.

7 June 1967: Advance to Romani. Action at Bir Gifgafa. Occupation of Sharm-el-Sheikh.

8 June 1967: Action near Nakhl. Israelis reach the Suez Canal. Fall of El Qantara.

CHAPTER VII: SINAI REVISITED

'If the principles of war were not immutable, and therefore to be learnt from the experience of the past, there would be little need of books on military history. The geography of a land determines the course of its wars, and a knowledge of previous campaigns serves to interpret the influence on strategy of the land's main topographical features.'
Colonel A. P. Wavell.[52]

Armies have been tramping up and down the *Darab es Sultani*[53] since the beginning of recorded history, making their way across the arid desert of Sinai in order to invade the Nile Delta or the fertile crescent of Palestine and Syria. Assyrian and Egyptian; Persian and Macedonian; Roman and Arab; Frenchman, Turk and Briton had all passed that way before in 1956 General Moshe Dayan launched the Israeli Army on the first of its two modern *blitzkriegs*.

The Sinai Peninsula is a triangle 240 miles long from north to south, and about 120 from east to west at its base. The northern zone consists firstly of a belt of sand dunes, along the coast. They are extremely heavy going and in the 1914–18 war were considered impassable for wheeled horse-drawn vehicles. Then there is a relatively narrow coastal plain, south of the dunes, varying in width from about five to fifteen miles. The central zone, an inhospitable rocky plateau, rises to some 3,000 feet. Here the going is firm, but it is not easy to dig in. The southern zone is a wilderness of rugged mountains some of

---

[52] Later Field Marshal Viscount Wavell, in *The Palestine Campaigns*, p. 3.
[53] The Royal Road.

them 10,000 feet high. Along the Mediterranean coast there is brackish water at a depth of twelve to eighteen inches, but elsewhere there is no water supply that will support an army. The population may number 100,000, mostly nomadic Bedouin. El Arish and Nakhl in the south are the only places of any size. Biting winds and sandstorms in the winter, and a blistering sun in the summer, add to the charms of this delectable area. The only thing that can be said for it is that it is not a bad place for armies to fight, since they can't do much harm except to each other.

Napoleon, who had passed through the Sinai Desert on his way to his first defeat, before Acre, was impressed — 'Of all obstacles which can cover the frontiers of Empires, a desert, similar to this, is incontestably the greatest.' He may well have been right, but in fact, as we have seen, the peninsula has been crossed by armies not once but many times. It is simply a question of good preparation and organization, and in this sphere no army is more capable than that of Israel. With relatively recent experience to guide them it was evident that they could solve the organizational problem of getting their army to the Suez Canal. To cross 120 miles of desert, though not easy, is not indeed a particularly difficult feat for a modern mechanized army, especially one with air superiority. It seems not unlikely that the Egyptians questioned Field Marshal Montgomery on this point after that famous lecture on El Alamein at their Higher Military Academy. Perhaps he told them that the Axis army there had been starved of petrol at the end of a long and vulnerable L. of C. But then Rommel's El Alamein position was 550 miles from his base at Benghazi and 1100 from his main base at Tripoli. The commanders of the forward Egyptian divisions, assured of adequate air cover and with at most only 120 miles of L. of C., must have felt reassured.

The Egyptians, like the Israelis, must have learned something from the wars of 1948 and 1956. One may not entertain a very high opinion of the Egyptian officer corps, but it is sensible to recognize that some of its officers did well in 1948, Nasser himself, Neguib and Hakim Amer to name only the more obvious cases. The latter could certainly lay on a fire-plan as he proved at Yad Mordechai and Nitzanim, and if he took a sledgehammer to crack a nut that only proves that he understood the capabilities of the men entrusted to his command[54]. It would be unreasonable to suppose that the departure of King Farouk and the Pashas led to no improvement in the Egyptian army, though certainly it made nothing like the progress that its opponents made between 1948 and 1967.

Whatever one may think of Egyptian officers as warriors there is no reason to doubt their ability as students. Fed by *Al Ahram* and Cairo Radio they develop, no doubt, prejudices that we would deplore, but the mental equipment of Arab or Egyptian is potentially as good as anyone else's. It follows that they made a serious study of the 1956 campaign, and especially of the interesting Operation Orders of 5 and 25 October printed as appendices to Moshe Dayan's *Diary of The Sinai*

---

[54] At Yad Mordechai a garrison equivalent to an ill-armed company held up a brigade group for a week and then broke out. The commander, one Grischa, had served as a sergeant in the Buffs in Italy. At Nitzanim a strong Egyptian force with guns and tanks overran two platoons' worth of Jewish settlers, taking most of a day to do it. The Israelis lost 3 women and some 30 men killed, and the Egyptians had about 50 casualties. I was able to visit both places in October 1966 and heard the story from survivors. Both these *kibbutzim* have, not without reason, become places of pilgrimage for the Israelis of today.

Campaign. Indeed the Egyptian dispositions of May 1967 were skilfully designed to cover against precisely the plan of attack there detailed. Since, despite first appearances, the Israelis did *not* try to make History repeat itself, the plan of 1956, which General Dayan had so conveniently handed to General Mortagi's staff on a plate, served as a Deception Plan. The Egyptians, like a pugilist who has just been hit in the guts, had both fists ready to parry the next punch at the same target. But this time they took a right to the chin.

By 5 June Egypt had something like 100,000 men, seven divisions, massed in the Sinai Desert. In the north were four infantry divisions, liberally supported by tanks, and dug in, in what General Beaufre[55] calls '*un curieux style sovietique*'. This was made up of successive, but, broadly speaking, discontinuous, lines of defence. To the south, facing the Negev, the armoured corps was deployed in depth. This concentration called for a considerable administrative effort: piped water, supply depots and all the impedimenta of desert warfare, modern version — at least World War Two version.

Israel, with Syria and Jordan to reckon with, had been able to allot no more than three divisions and two independent brigades to General S. Gavish (G.O.C. Southern Command). The Israelis have not revealed their strength, but it was probably about 44,000 men.

Gavish and his commanders were an interesting group. He himself was ex-Palmach[56], and had been Director of Military Training.

---

[55] General André Beaufre commanded the French forces at Suez in 1956. He visited Israel immediately after the 1967 campaign and contributed an extremely valuable article to *Paris-Match* (June, 1967). General Beaufre is director of the French Institute of Strategic Studies and author of three important books on Modern Strategy.

Tal served in the British Army in the Palestine Regiment, where he had his first experience of 'armour' as a sergeant in a Bren Carrier. A perfectionist, as Director of Armour, he had infused a tremendous spirit into his command, which, according to one British observer (October 1966) was 'almost too anxious for war…' After training hard for years the Jewish armoured corps wanted to try it all out in practice.

Avraham Yoffe had served in the Royal Artillery. A reserve officer he was the oldest of Gavish's senior commanders, and had become Director of National Parks. His men were all reservists too. An Israeli colonel characterized him in a letter to the author as 'Ex Brit. Army officer, jolly Jumbo type'.

Aric Sharon, then Director of Military Training, took the southern division into action. He has been described by a Jewish officer as 'a fighting animal' on the strength of his many raids. To the present writer, who has known him, on and off, since 1957, when Sharon was at the Staff College, Camberley, he appears to be far more than that. A distinguished fighting record *need* not be taken as positive proof of mental deficiency. Sharon is certainly a warlike figure, the born leader one hears about but so seldom meets. But his plans are the result of much thought and study and he has a mind receptive to ideas — even other peoples'.

The main phases of General Gavish's campaign will be clear, it is hoped, from the accompanying plan, which is based on a map prepared by the Israeli General Staff and entitled 'I.D.F. Routes of Advance. 5th–10th June 1967'.[57]

---

[56] Palmach means Spearhead and was the elite of the Israeli Army in the 1948 fighting.

[57] I wish to express my gratitude to Brigadier-General Zamir, Israeli Military Attaché in London, for providing me with copies of this map and much other documentation.

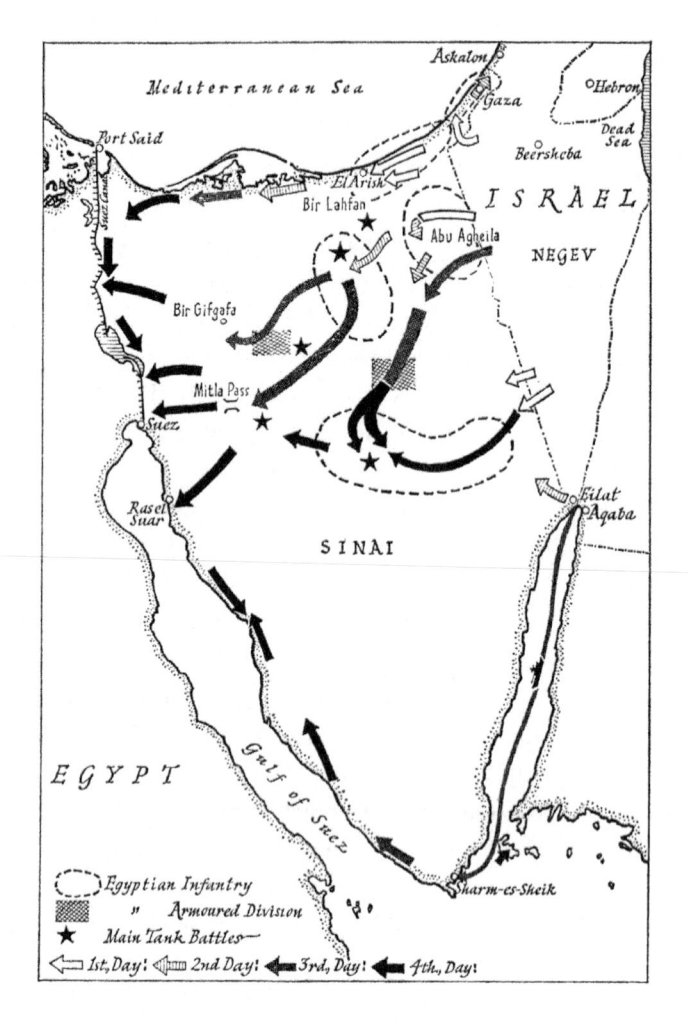

General Rabin's plan was to develop in three phases.

Phase One. Penetration of the Egyptian defences at two of their strongest points: El Arish and Abu Agheila.

Phase Two. Move forward to the mountains east of the Suez Canal and block the escape routes.

Phase Three. Destruction of the Egyptian army in Sinai.

It looks simple enough on paper, though it was bound to mean hard fighting. It can be said that the plan fulfils rather well the classic concept for a major battle.

Writing of the 1914–18 war Field Marshal Wavell tells us: 'A great battle, as contemplated by Field Service Regulations, normally comprised three phases. The first phase was the collision of the advanced troops, under cover of which the rival commanders developed their plan of action, while their armies gradually deployed their full strength.' In Gavish's campaign all this phase had already taken place *before* 5 June.

'The second phase, when battle had been fairly joined by the main forces, was the struggle to obtain fire superiority and to exhaust the enemy's reserves in preparation for the final attack.' This phase coincides with the battles Tal and Sharon fought on 5 and 6 June.

'The third phase (was) the decisive great attack or counter-attack and the exploitation of success, once the enemy's line has broken...'[58] This was the fighting on 7 and 8 June. Considering that armour was in its infancy when Wavell wrote one may observe that the methods of conducting war change rather less rapidly than some modern students of war suppose. On the face of it one might expect that the Rabin-Gavish plan was bound to bring on a Second rather than a first World War Battle, an Alamein rather than a Megiddo, if only because the Egyptians were so numerous, and had so much armour. But Montgomery has told us that his plan for Alamein 'was to hold off, or contain, the enemy armour while we carried out a methodical destruction of the infantry divisions holding the defensive system. These unarmoured divisions would be destroyed by means of a crumbling process, the enemy being attacked from flank and rear and cut off from their supplies.

---

[58] *The Palestine Campaigns*, pp. 14 and 15.

These operations would be carefully organized from a series of firm bases and would be within the capabilities of my troops'.[59] Montgomery considered that many of his commanders were 'above their ceiling, and few were good trainers...' The Israeli leaders suffered from no such inhibitions, and so we find little of El Alamein in their thinking, but something of O'Connor's offensive of December 1940.

In its broad lines the Israeli plan worked out well, and to describe it in a purely chronological fashion would merely obscure the lessons. It seems preferable to analyse some of the more significant features of the fighting.

To begin with the break-in was evidently a triple penetration. On Yoffe's front deception was obtained by crossing terrain which in that general's words 'every officer will tell you is not possible'. The Egyptians had failed to block this route.

The plan to break up the enemy's strongest positions first was perfectly sound since the early collapse of a fortress in which the defender trusts may well shake the rest of his army. The early capture of the Belgian fortress of Eben Emael in 1940 is an example that springs to mind.

Again the early attack on El Arish was clearly a shrewd stroke for it is an important station on the railway from El Qantara to Gaza. Even if their agents did not tell them, the Israeli staff would easily work out that it was an important supply point for most of the Egyptian divisions in Sinai.

There was hard fighting everywhere but the main armoured force, Rabin's 'mailed fist' thought to have numbered 250–300 tanks, was entrusted, not unnaturally, to Tal. His method of operating was to pierce the Egyptian front line, penetrate deep, then turn and attack from the rear. The comparison with

---

[59] Memoirs of Field-Marshal Montgomery.

O'Connor's attack on the Italian forts, Sofafi East, Sofafi West and Nibeiwa (7 December 1940) is striking.

Here is Tal's description of his part in the first stage of the offensive:

'The objectives of my division were to penetrate the fortified lines of the First Division (reinforced by the Palestinian Brigade) in the Rafa area, and to cut through the concrete fortification-positions at Sheikh Zuwaib and Jirdi in order to capture El Arish. Following up on that we were to continue on the one hand along the northern axis to the Canal, and on the other to cut through another line of fortifications at Bir Lahfan in order to advance in the direction of Bir Gifgafa and from there to the Suez Canal. Our main purpose, of course, was not to occupy as much territory as possible, but to destroy the enemy's divisions. We knew that the first breakthrough action at Rafa would actually be a trial of strength between us and the Egyptian army, which we had not clashed with for more than ten years. It was clear to all our soldiers and officers that the action would have to be carried out regardless of losses. The enemy lines stretched back in depth for 12 kilometres, with fortified positions on either side; anti-tank guns, tanks and mines. We made a frontal attack on the right flank next to the sea coast not far from Rafa. On the left we effected a breakthrough coming out of the sands and on to the enemy's rear positions which were supported by artillery. The moment the first breakthrough on the western flank was effected our tank force, without waiting for the final outcome, broke through the Jirdi position with its concrete fortifications and reached the approaches of El Arish. And so, on the first evening, we attained our first decisive success, with the total destruction of the enemy's Seventh Division and moved our tanks into El Arish.'

The dash of the Israelis sometimes landed them in trouble. Their charge through the Palestinians at Khan Yunis cost them 35 tank commanders, including a battalion commander, thanks to their habit of fighting with their turrets open. One suspects, however, that under the circumstances such tactics may actually have been less costly than groping about shut down and blind.

To the Egyptians' credit it must be said that there was some very hard fighting indeed. One of Tal's tank battalions destroyed twenty Stalin tanks, then some guns which they had been protecting, and pushing on destroyed a further twenty Egyptian tanks. Soon after Tal spoke on the air to one of his battalion commanders who had got cut off and could hear him firing his machine-gun while he was talking. Still the general had kept a brigade up his sleeve and was able to sort this situation out by means of a swift turning movement.

The Egyptians defending Rafa put up a stiff resistance. One brigade is reported to have had the very high number of 1,000 men killed before they were overrun, fighting one of Tal's brigades practically to a standstill. At one time this formation had only one company capable of further operation without rest or reorganization. At this juncture another Egyptian brigade gave its position away by trying to shoot up a helicopter, which was landing to collect casualties. The Israeli brigade commander then led his one remaining tank company against this formation. His success may be attributed to the fact that it was now night, and as General Sharon said later: 'The Egyptians do not like fighting at night nor do they enjoy hand-to-hand combat — we specialize in both.'

A two-hour battle apparently cost the Egyptians another 1,500 dead. The Israeli brigade, operating 'regardless of cost' as they had been briefed to, had lost many casualties including 70 dead. Tal's description of the El Arish-Rafa fighting as 'a brutal battle' is certainly justified. He observed that while the Egyptian tanks gave their positions away with their opening rounds, the anti-tank guns, firing salvoes from well-concealed concrete bunkers, were almost impossible to spot so that few were knocked out by tank fire. The Israeli tanks advanced on the flashes and crushed them. One would imagine that this solution, though effective, must have been costly.

It would be very wrong to suppose that the Israelis knew only how 'to get stuck in' and how to make armoured cavalry charges. They could also lay on what Tal calls a 'sophisticated attack'. This involved halting as soon as the leading tank battalion had made contact to make use of their good gunnery and the superior range of the 105mm guns which the British Centurion tank mounts. This was capable of knocking out anti-tank guns sited in concrete bunkers or T-54 tanks at a range of about 4,000 yards. The Defence Correspondent of *The Times*[60], who saw the latest Russian tanks knocked out by shots right through their front armour, said that the 105mm gun had 'certainly been proved in a harder school than any tank gun of the West', including the Patton which the Americans had publicised so much after the Kashmir war.

When his men had gained fire superiority Tal began to work a second battalion round the Egyptians eastern flank where many got stuck in the dunes. The advance of another battalion relieved them from their plight, since the Egyptians, as troops in a defensive position so often will when their flanks are threatened, retreated. They had lost fifteen tanks, thirty anti-tank guns and two anti-aircraft guns, *without causing a single*

---

[60] Charles Douglas-Home in a lecture at The Royal United Service Institution on 13 July 1967.

casualty. It was not courage but expertise that the Egyptian soldier lacked.

If it fell to Tal to play the main role in this campaign. Sharon too had his opportunity to display once more his remarkable tactical skill when he cracked the Egyptian position at Abu Agheila. This was a good example of the Soviet-style defence system criticised by General Beaufre. Sharon commented: 'That is convenient for us since we try to avoid frontal attacks.' Having just returned from the 25th anniversary celebrations at Dieppe one sees his point...[61] Like a good commando raider he briefed his officers on a sand-table, which was the more necessary since he had decided upon a night attack. Only a commander confident that his men were in a high state of training would have ventured such an assault. His plan, which seems to fall into six phases, was full of interesting features.

Phase One. Concentrated barrage by six artillery regiments.

Phase Two. Reconnaissance groups cut off Egyptian position from the rear to prevent reinforcement.

Phase Three. Tank attack on the rear of the enemy position.

Phase Four. Attack on Abu Agheila from the north, by paratroopers landed behind the enemy lines by helicopter in order to silence the Egyptian artillery.

Phase Five. Infantry assault on left (northern) Egyptian flank to clear the front line trenches and permit engineers to make lanes through the minefields.

Phase Six. Tanks break in to the main fortified position.

Had Sharon produced such a plan when he was a student at the Staff College at Camberley in 1957 some at least of the

---

[61] On 19 August 1942 the 2nd Canadian Division, less three battalions, was invited to capture the town of Dieppe in daylight, without serious naval gunfire support or a preliminary air bombardment. The raid was repulsed with considerable loss.

Directing Staff would have suffered strokes. But if it seems confusing it had the virtue that it also confused the Egyptians.

The plan involved a long approach march and though during the first part the troops rode in buses, the sand dunes became too soft, and the infantry had to do the last ten miles on foot, arriving in their forming up place under cover of darkness.

Phase Two went more or less according to plan, though not without resistance; so did the helicopter landing. Sharon pointed out that it is much more accurate and speedy to position troops than to drop them by parachute. Not only do they not get so dispersed, but they can be taken away again.

By 2200 hours a furious battle was in progress, and the Egyptians were making the area 'as light as day' with their explosive and incendiary shells. At 2200 Gavish's HQ suggested postponing the attack till next day when air support would be available. Sharon, however, considered that even with air support such a heavily fortified position would be impregnable by daylight. His men's morale influenced him. 'I had seen the confidence in their faces and knew they were ready to go. I could not keep them waiting. I was sure we could take it.' His attack began at 2245 when, for half an hour, his six regiments of artillery brought down the most tremendous barrage general Sharon had ever seen. Then the paratroopers and a tank regiment NW of the El Arish road began the assault with an attack on the Egyptian rear. Almost immediately after the armoured brigade began to move up through smoke and dust so thick that they could not fire.

When at 2315 the artillery ceased fire, the tanks opened up and the infantry went in. Each battalion had been issued with 50 torches, red, green, and blue respectively, so that they could signal progress to the tanks. Searchlights lit up the whole target area. By 0030 (6 June) the Egyptian artillery fire was fading away but though the general reported successes at 0300 the tank fighting was not over until 0600. Sharon will be believed when he asserts that this attack was the most complicated ever carried out by the Israeli army. He ascribes his victory to his men's complete confidence that they could take the position. And in the upshot the casualties were not by any means prohibitive. There is no doubt that well-trained troops have a decided advantage at night. The truth of this is amply demonstrated by various operations of World War Two, such as the capture by the First Commando Brigade of the Angouville Heights during the advance to the Seine in August 1944.[62]

Night training is unattractive to peacetime soldiers, but not, it seems, in the Israeli Army.

Battles are naturally more interesting when we know accurately the breakdown of the forces engaged. But the Israelis are not exactly forthcoming as to such details. We know that in the campaign the Israelis were outnumbered by more than two to one. But were the odds as heavy in the actual battles? It is unlikely. As we shall see Abd el Naby's brigade, to name but one, never got into action, it seems likely that by concentrating their divisions the Israeli commanders succeeded in building up a local superiority in actual combat, and so succeeded in defeating the Egyptians in detail. It was not simply a question of better morale, better training and better shooting, but of better tactics.

Fortunately the strength of Sharon's attack on Abu Agheila can be worked out with some precision. He had an armoured brigade; at least one infantry brigade; a reconnaissance group, which besides a regiment of tanks included heavy mortars and

---

[62] See *Clash by Night* by Brigadier D. Mills-Roberts, who commanded on that occasion.

engineers; a battalion of paratroopers and no less than six regiments of artillery. In round terms such a force could scarcely number less than 10,000 men.

The organization of brigades may be of interest to professional soldiers:

> H.Q.: Armoured: 1, Infantry: 1
> Signal company: Armoured: 1, Infantry: 1
> Tank regiments: Armoured: 2, Infantry: 0
> Infantry battalion[63]: Armoured: 1, Infantry: 3
> Reconnaissance company: Armoured: 1, Infantry: 1
> SP artillery regiment[64]: Armoured: 1, Infantry: 0
> 120mm mortar regiment[65]: Armoured: 0, Infantry: 1
> AA squadron[66]: Armoured: 1, Infantry: 0
> Engineer company: Armoured: 1, Infantry: 1 platoon
> Casualty Clearing station: Armoured: 1, Infantry: 1
> Quartermaster company (Supply and Transport): Armoured: 1, Infantry: 0
> Ordnance company: Armoured: 1, Infantry: 1 section
> Military Police Platoon: Armoured: 1, Infantry: 1

The paratroop battalion would have consisted of H.Q., a support company and four rifle companies, each approximately 113 strong. Since an Israeli parachute brigade of H.Q. and three battalions number about 3,000 all ranks, the battalion with Sharon probably mustered something like 700 men.

Since the Egyptians had locked up great numbers of men in their fortifications, it was possible for the Israelis, by manoeuvre and by a skilful selection of objectives, to build up the local superiority necessary to achieve a breakthrough. But

---

[63] Carried in armoured half-tracks.
[64] Not organic in peacetime.
[65] Obsolete.
[66] 12 mortars, carried in half-tracks.

this superiority was not, of course, a question so much of numbers, but of firepower wedded to intelligent tactics.

On rare occasions the Egyptians actually attempted a counter-attack. Tal describes how when his tanks took up a position at Bir Gifgafa in order to block their escape route towards the Canal the Egyptians, 'understanding the critical nature of this move, attempted to counter-attack in the direction of Bir Gifgafa, at the same time co-ordinating their attack with air support. This assault was repulsed, and we moved on to counter-attack. One of our forces was positioned at Bir Gifgafa and another on the southern flank. In this counter-attack we destroyed an Egyptian mechanised brigade which had massed for an additional counter-attack. This was effected during our deployment. At this stage, additional Egyptian forces, mainly T-55 tanks, were brought up from the Canal Zone in order to attempt to pull our "cork" out of the Bir Gifgafa bottleneck. However, one of our regiments had been positioned along this possible line of advance, in order to prevent just such a contingency. This was a regiment of light tanks, and it engaged in bitter fighting for over two hours with the enemy force of over sixty T-55 tanks. It was here that we incurred many casualties, particularly since, through a stroke of ill luck, our supply of mortar-shells and other explosives was blown up in the midst of our regiment. Nevertheless, our regiment held their ground and succeeded in maintaining their position blocking all passage to the enemy T-55s until our boys were reinforced by units we sent off at a later time'.

The advance on the central axis towards the Canal was not always swift... 'with the enemy attempting constant delaying action with a force of a hundred tanks — mainly T-55's. Our advance was slow at this stage: it took us six hours to cover five kilometres — but we managed to destroy some forty enemy tanks along this stretch. It was here that the enemy was broken and thus, by means of light reconnaissance units supported by a small number of tanks, we quickly reached the Canal. This battle along a very narrow axis which did not permit us to manoeuvre freely, in view of the sand dunes hemming us in, was conducted by sniping methods. Only three tanks led all the time, but their gunners were excellent and at ranges of 3,000, 2,000 and 1,000 metres we hit the enemy every time, even though they were always the first to fire, having positioned themselves in such a manner as to be able to sight us first.

'On the northern axis we advanced about half the way without any opposition, but during the second half of our advance we met a type of resistance similar to the one we encountered along the central axis, and adopted a similar manner of progress. At this stage, the Egyptians threw in their aircraft against us along the central axis, and for three hours there was fairly bitter fighting between their airplanes and our land forces. The Egyptians managed to hold up our advance for a short time, but finally our air force intervened and helped to turn the scales in our favour.'

The Egyptians can be criticised for neglecting to hold the Mitla Pass, by which at least part of their army would be compelled to withdraw in the event of defeat. It is nearly 15 miles long and in General Yoffe's words 'whoever commands the opening to the Pass is actually in command of all access to the Canal'. In 1956 the Pass was captured after hard fighting by Sharon and a battalion of paratroopers. An elementary knowledge of their recent military history should have warned the Egyptian commanders to secure this vital ground. Yoffe was ordered to race for the Pass and cut off any Egyptians retreating to the Canal. He arrived in time and thereafter remained on the defensive.

The capture of Sharm-el-Sheikh (7 June) was notable chiefly for the fact that the Israelis arrived to receive a tame surrender from a garrison whose officers had departed, after delivering suitable exhortations, the previous day.

Early in the morning of 8 June, after their first night's sleep since they crossed the frontier, Sharon's division found themselves confronted by the Stalin tanks of the 125th Brigade. They had been abandoned — undamaged.

When the fighting was over its commander, Brigadier Abd El-Naby, talked to General Sharon. He had been alarmed on the night 6–7 June by the noise of armour moving up from the west. It turned out to be Egyptian tanks of whose approach he had not been warned. On the next night he was ordered to withdraw, but as nothing was said about destroying his tanks, he left them intact and made for Bir Thamada in half-tracks. The brigade ran into a roadblock, broke up, and began to make for the Mitla Pass. 'I lost all my order at the Mitla,' the Brigadier told an American correspondent. 'Everyone wanted to flee for his own skin. All vehicles were abandoned and the men set off on foot to cross the mountains to the west.' ... 'I lost my luggage, which I bought in London a month before, and my transistor radio.'

Sharon had some pungent comments on this interview: 'I have had long talks with my men about the war and the fighting that was to come. I have great respect for my men while the Egyptian commanders despise their own troops. I think the Egyptian soldiers are very good. They are simple and ignorant but they are strong and they are disciplined. They are good gunners, good diggers and good shooters — but their officers are shit, they can fight only according to what they planned before. Once we had broken through, except for the minefield between Bir Hassneh and Nakhl, which was probably there before the war, the Egyptian officers placed no mines and laid no ambushes to block our line of advance. But some of the soldiers, particularly at the Mitla where we had blocked their line of retreat, fought to the death in an attempt to break westwards to the Canal. Just as they did at Faluga in 1948, where, incidentally, Nasser was fighting as a junior officer.' At Kusseima Sharon saw an Egyptian soldier sitting at the roadside crying, 'They left me, they left me.'

Yoffe describes a strange manoeuvre which he was compelled to carry out in the Mitla Pass on the morning of 8 June. His leading brigade had been fighting without rest for 72 hours and the men were dead tired.

He was compelled to relieve his leading brigade while it was actually in action, the tanks firing all the time while the takeover was going on.

How many of the Israeli soldiers who fought their way across the Sinai Desert in June 1967 had already passed that way in 1956? Very few, one imagines, of the junior officers or of the rank and file. Commanders of the rank of major and above, a handful of senior N.C.O.s: these, it may be supposed, were the veterans. It was a new generation that was now proving itself under fire. General Sharon, looking into his soldiers' eyes, had confidence in them. Not all the older generation had his sound instinctive judgment. They did not know their men. Eshkol himself, at 71, seems to have been somewhat surprised that they made good. He is reported as saying after the fighting: 'This very youth, some of whom were the subject of criticism as a result of their way of life and their lack of social values, was discovered as a wonderful youth'... We in Britain should recognize the attitude. In the '30s the generation that fought the First World War had but a poor opinion of the generation that was to fight the Second.

At what stage, one wonders, did the Egyptian High Command appreciate that its Air Force was broken, that its forces in Sinai would now be fighting without air cover? In theory this should have been clear by about 11 in the morning of 5 June. By that time the commander-in-chief of the Egyptian army in Sinai should have had sufficient information on this vital subject to be able to make a decision as to his next move. In fact wishful thinking, failures of communications or a desire to conceal disaster may have obscured the picture. We do not yet know exactly when it was borne in upon General Abdul Muhsin Kamal Mortagi that the air battle was lost. It seems not unlikely that the awful truth was known about midday on 5 June. By this time the pressure of the Israeli armoured thrusts was already making itself felt, and Mortagi really only had two alternatives: to stand and fight where he was, or to withdraw behind the Suez Canal. If he had ever contemplated an actual invasion of Israel the time for an offensive was now past. In fact Mortagi, a moderate and reasonable man, is reported as saying that while Egypt did not accept the state of Israel she would definitely not attack her.

But if the general was inhibited by his private opinions from contemplating an offensive, he was probably prevented by the dictator behind him from considering an early withdrawal. A withdrawal begun on the night of 5/6 June would have been an extremely difficult test of Egyptian staff work, and followed up by such thrustful opponents could have deteriorated into a rout every bit as bad as the disaster that in fact came to pass. There may be those who credit the Egyptian staff with the ability to plan at short notice a withdrawal of this sort, and to transmit the necessary orders to the various formations. But even supposing this to have been possible would Nasser have permitted it so early in the proceedings? Remembering the late Adolf Hitler's reactions to similar proposals this appears highly improbable. It seems likely that the suggestion of a withdrawal, intended to save something from the wreck, would have been taken by the dictator for infirmity of purpose — not an unnatural reaction.

It may be too that General Mortagi's character and training were such as to decide him to dig his heels in and hang on. His reputation is that of a calm, sensible professional infantry man, with little interest in politics. He was at one time senior to Nasser, and a member of King Farouk's Bodyguard. He attended the staff college (1952), a long course in Russia (1956), was chief of the Army Directorate of Training (1959) and commander of U.A.R. forces in the Yemen (1964). One may assume that his Russian training would predispose him in favour of sticking to the Kursk-like fortifications of El Arish and Agheila, and hoping that all would come right in the end. There is evidence from Cyprus and elsewhere of a breakdown in Egyptian wireless communications. It may be that an orderly withdrawal to the Canal was not really practical after the very first night of the war, but this is speculation.

The Israeli victory in the Sinai campaign was a very fine feat of arms. So much is obvious. There are those who regard it as being the finest feat of arms of this century; the best example yet seen of the *blitzkrieg*. It seems almost churlish to mention the considerations which may lead one to modify this view.

To revert to Colonel Burne's *Strands of War* there can be no question that the Israelis had the advantage in the quality and capability of their commander and of their troops, and in morale. In resources the Egyptians had a distinct advantage, at least on paper, but it did not suffice to outweigh the other three factors.

The Israelis knew that speed was essential, not only for military but for political reasons. They were afraid that a ceasefire might be imposed before the task was done. They knew from the experience of 1956 that a speedy knockout blow was not an impossibility given the right opponents: the Egyptians. And so a wondering world witnessed the swiftest *blitzkrieg* yet. How did it come to pass? Why were the Israelis able to smite the Egyptians so much more quickly than the Germans had defeated the Poles in 1939 or the Allies in 1940, or than O'Connor had routed Graziani? It is partly a question of national characteristics. The Poles though armed with obsolescent weapons were tough and patriotic. They gave the Germans a run for their money. The French army of 1940 was poorly commanded, badly deployed, and its units varied in quality. But the B.E.F. was tenacious enough, and, though it is too seldom remembered, some of the French meant business.[67] If O'Connor had been outnumbered by two instead of ten to one, it is reasonable to suppose that he would have dealt with Graziani even faster than he did.

Distance comes into it too — rather obviously: to cross the Sinai Desert is only a matter of 120 miles. Then it must be remembered that a large part of the German army of 1939 and 1940 was horse-drawn, which does not exactly contribute to the pace of the *blitzkrieg*.

It is true that the Israeli commanders were absolutely clear in their minds as to the way they meant to attain their aims; hence the beautiful certainty of their moves. There were none of the

---

[67] Twelve French fighter pilots fought with the R.A.F. in the Battle of Britain and only two survived. Men like these can hardly be accused of poor morale.

doubts and fears that assailed some of the German commanders — men like von Kleist and even von Rundstedt — when Guderian launched off into the blue in 1940.

But having said that let us be frank and say that the Israelis were fortunate in their opponents. They are certainly a match, under current circumstances, for any of their neighbours. It would be a pity, however, if elation deluded them into supposing that they are absolutely invincible. On the other hand one cannot fail to be impressed by the way they have improved in recent years. During the Jerusalem Incident of 1954 they only succeeded in wounding one soldier of the 9th Regiment, in some 48 hours' shooting, which led me to comment that 'we were not up against the Hermann Goering Division' — a remark that rankled with my old friend Robert Henriques, and on which several Israeli officers questioned me during my visit last year. It seems the shaft went home! Perhaps, all unintentionally, I did the Israelis a good turn. Who knows? It may have persuaded some of them to zero their rifles. However that may be, it is certain that there has been a steady improvement over the years. While Weizman was building up the Air Force to its present brilliant state of training, Rabin, Tal, Sharon and the rest, were forging the weapon that was to deny Nasser his prey.

The capture of the Gaza Strip presented the Israelis with a propaganda success. At the Egyptian intelligence bureau documents were captured minutes before its personnel managed to burn them. The contents — somewhat singed — are evidence that the Egyptians no longer cared if their sabotage activities provoked war with Israel.[68] It will be

---

[68] Brigadier Z. Zamir had the kindness to send me a brochure entitled 'Top Secret Operational Files of the Egyptian Intelligence Reveals:

recalled that since early in the year President Nasser had permitted the miserable Shuqairy (Head of the Palestine Liberation Army) to step up his raiding activities.

Besides concentrating on the training of 41 *Fedayeen* battalion, Egyptian intelligence officers had attended meetings at Damascus in February and April with members of El Fatah terrorist organization, Syrian intelligence officers and Shuqairy's 'heroes of the Return'. These meetings discussed the possible activities of the various sabotage organizations, working across from the Syrian, Lebanese or Jordanian borders, while 41 *Fedayeen* operated from Egyptian territory.

The Egyptians had little confidence in the operational standards of their allies, and were determined to have absolute control over the sabotage activities directed from their own territory.

Files on the various Israeli settlements, including Ofakim, Magen, Sderot and Zimim, were prepared.

On 28 May 1967 Nasser held a press conference at which he declared: 'I support the full right of the Palestinians to embark by themselves upon a war of liberation for the return of their rights and country.' In consequence several raids were actually carried out during early June 1967 before the campaign started.

The tasks assigned included the harassment of settlements, the burning of stores, garages and sheep-pens and the destruction of water pipelines.

The orders for these raids are interesting. The description of the settlements at Ofakim and Magen is very well detailed. On the other hand it is quite obvious that nothing more than a pinprick raid was contemplated. In each case the raiders' main weapons were to be five Karl Gustav sub-machineguns and

---

The Egyptian Intelligence in Gaza Strip Made Preparations Sabotage of Israeli Settlements.' July 1967.

one 7.92 light machinegun, from which it is evident that only six men were to take part. It was not, perhaps, a very ambitious programme, but at least it indicates that after ten years of lassitude the Egyptians, determined to wrest the leadership of the Arab world from the Syrians, were prepared to provoke the wrath of the Israelis.

The four days' fighting in the Sinai Peninsula cost the Egyptians over 700 Russian tanks, mainly T-54s and T-55s, some of them with very low mileages on their speedometers and still painted bottle-green. The Israelis admitted the loss of 61 tanks.

The Israelis captured nearly 5,000 Egyptian officers. The men, what were left of them, were allowed to make for the Canal. Some reached it only to be machine-gunned by their own side. Some were lucky and received water or a lift to Qantara from their enemies. Others rest where they fell in the parched desert where their President sent them.

CHAPTER VIII CHRONOLOGY

13 November 1966: The Samu Raid.
24 May–4 June 1967: Iraqi troops arrive in Jordan.
30 May 1967: Cairo. President Nasser kisses King Hussein.
3 June 1967: Israelis hear that an Egyptian 'Commando' has arrived in Amman.
0745 5 June 1967: Israeli air strikes against Egypt.
a.m. 5 June 1967: Mr. Eshkol informs King Hussein that Israel will 'not initiate any action whatsoever against Jordan'.
c. 0830 5 June 1967: Jerusalem. Sporadic shelling.
Before 1030 5 June 1967: Jordanians take Government House (Cairo Radio).
1035 5 June 1967: Egyptian Air Force virtually destroyed.
By 1130 5 June 1967: Jordanian front. Firing general.
1200 5 June 1967: The United Nations ask for a ceasefire.
1220–1240 5 June 1967: Ineffective Jordanian air strikes on Netanya and near Tel Aviv.
1410 5 June 1967: Jerusalem. Israeli brigade commander reports occupation of Government House by the Jordanians.
1425 5 June 1967: General Narkiss ordered to counter-attack in the Jerusalem area.
1550 5 June 1967: Government House taken by the Israelis.
1730 5 June 1967: Jerusalem. Israeli attack begins.
By 1920 5 June 1967: Abdul Aziz hill, Radar and Bet Iksa taken.
Night 5 June 1967: The capture of Jenin.
0220 6 June 1967: Jerusalem. Israeli paratroop brigade attacks.
0345 6 June 1967: Police School taken.

c. 0600 6 June 1967: Sheikh Jarrah taken. Israeli armoured brigade cuts Jerusalem-Ramallah road. Qalqilya, Latrun and Ramallah taken.

0830–1015 7 June 1967: Israelis take the Old City of Jerusalem. Fall of Nablus, Tulkarm, Jericho and Hebron.

CHAPTER VIII: JORDAN DISMEMBERED

'Your men are making history — what is going on in Sinai is nothing compared to this.'

General Shlomo Goren.
Chief Rabbi of the Israel Army.[69]

'We went to fight men. We met only steel.'

Jordanian Soldier.

Palestine, the area comprising the Kingdom of Jordan and the Republic of Israel, is a territory rather smaller than Wales. From Amman to the Mediterranean Sea is only 75 miles; from Dan to Beersheba it is only 150 miles. These distances give a good idea of the main theatres of the fighting between Israel and Jordan, for there was no fighting in the Eilat-Aqaba area. For such a small country Palestine is remarkable for the variety of its climate and terrain.

Looked at from a military point of view the country falls into four regions:

1. The Plains held in May 1967 by Israel
2. The Judaean Hills divided in May 1967
3. The Jordan Valley divided in May 1967
4. Transjordan held in May 1967 by Jordan

The Plains, Philistia, Sharon and Esdraelon are the Heartland of Israel. The distance from the Mediterranean Sea to the main range of the Judaean Hills varies from about ten to fifteen

---

[69] To General Narkiss. Midnight, 5 June 1967.

miles. North to south up the plains runs the ancient highway linking the cradles of civilization in the valleys of the Nile and the Euphrates. The whole area lies open to an enemy established in the Judaean Hills, where in 1967 the Israelis had only one foothold, their salient at Jerusalem.

The Judaean Hills are a relatively narrow range, running north and south and averaging a height of 2,400 feet, but rising in various places to 3,500. Owing to the spurs running out from the main ridge it is, generally speaking, much easier for an army to operate from east to west, than from north to south.

The Jordan Valley is below sea level for its entire length. At Lake Tiberias[70] it is 680 feet below and at the Dead Sea, 1,300. It is a great trench dividing the Judaean Range from the Mountains of Moab in Transjordan. The passage of the river itself is not particularly formidable since it can be forded in a number of places, but the steepness of the descent by the few roads down the mountains on either side renders the valley a serious obstacle to an army moving east or west. In 1967 the fact that the Israelis were already established in the valley as far south as Beisan was a strategic factor of prime importance.

Transjordan is the tableland between the River Jordan and the Desert, which begins just beyond the line of the railway running down via Damascus and Amman to Medina — the old Hejaz Railway which Lawrence of Arabia used to prey upon. It is on the whole a poor country and is now all that remains of the Hashemite Kingdom of Jordan.

In 1954 the garrison of the Old City of Jerusalem, which I then commanded, was the 9th Regiment of the Arab Legion. It was our task not only to man the defences of the city, but to work on the existing posts, which required improvement, and to

---

[70] Or the Sea of Galilee or Lake Kinneret, whichever you prefer.

prepare plans against every eventuality. In the absence of the brigadier I used to command the brigade and this gave me a good idea of the country from Ramallah to Hebron.

The chief difficulty under which we laboured in those days was shortage of manpower. The Arab Legion then had only three infantry brigades, one of which was always stationed on the West Bank of the River Jordan.

But by 1967 the Jordan Army had grown to nine brigades, three of them armoured. There were at least two brigades in the Jerusalem area. Even so the Arab position was not particularly attractive.

When in December 1917 Allenby's army attacked Jerusalem it struck in from the West — the direction from which the Israelis would come — taking first of all the outlying high ground at Nebi Samwil, the vantage point from which, long ago, Richard Coeur de Lion had his only glimpse of the Holy City. Pushing on the British took the Tel el Ful, severing the Turkish communications with the north *via* Ramallah and Nablus. An army strong enough to spare a brigade for the defence of the Nebi Samwil area might have a good chance of holding Jerusalem. This the Jordanians could not afford either in 1954, when only two battalions could be spared for the Jerusalem area, or in 1967.

The position had other weaknesses. First there was a Jewish enclave *behind* the Jordanian lines, in the old Hebrew University, strong buildings held by a company of 'police'. This foothold on Mount Scopus backing the Jordanian front line at half a mile's range was a constant headache to the commanders charged with the defence of the city. Then to the south, commanding the Bethlehem road, was another enclave, a neutral one, the former Government House (Dar el Mandub) built for the British High Commissioner and occupied since the expiration of the Mandate by the local H.Q. of U.N.O. In 1967 this was the residence of General Odd Bull.

The Old City itself, protected on the west by the solidly built Citadel, though only garrisoned by one infantry company in my time, was nevertheless a formidable position. Suleiman the Magnificent had built well and since we appreciated that respect for the Holy Places would prevent the Israelis from using all their ironmongery in an attack upon it — which indeed proved to be the case — I always felt confident that whatever else happened we ought to be able to hang on to the Old City, or at least the Citadel, until U.N.O. or the superpowers should impose a ceasefire. It is greatly to the credit of the Israelis that they battered their way in so swiftly.

Certainly they went about it the right way: that is to say by a pincers movement, through the suburbs ending up with an assault on the least well-defended side, through St. Stephen's Gate.

During the last four months of my service with the Arab Legion the 9th Regiment was responsible for guarding the frontier from a point south of Beisan to Jenin and down almost to Tulkarm, an area for which a division would scarcely be an adequate garrison.

From a commanding officer's point of view it was an interesting job. Being strung out over a wide area one had to travel about daily and got to see a great deal of the country. Of course, if there had been a serious attack it might have been extremely embarrassing. But there wasn't and in fact our main problem turned out to be Internal Security in the wake of the ill-starred British attempt to induce Jordan to join the Baghdad Pact.

The main defensive positions in the North were Jenin and Tubas, Tulkarm and Nablus.

On 13 November 1966 the Israelis attacked Samu, 15 kilometres south of Hebron. The attacking force seems to have been a parachute battalion supported by tanks and engineers, and with air cover. The platoon in the area was quickly overrun, and an infantry company which was rushed down to relieve the place was ambushed. The Israelis demolished Samu and neighbouring villages and withdrew. Hunters of the Royal Jordanian Air Force engaged the Israelis despite odds of three or four to one, and one was shot down near the Dead Sea.

After the raid Jordan was subjected to constant Arab and Egyptian radio propaganda against the Hashemite regime. As after Qibya (1953) rioting and demonstrations followed, involving the Jordan Arab Army in Internal Security duties. Despite considerable provocation from civilians and propaganda the Army and the police remained steady.

At a time when the Syrians were constantly raiding their borders the Israelis had retaliated against Jordan. What could this mean except that Israel was determined to drive Jordan into the arms of Syria and Egypt? This was my conclusion at the time, and this no doubt was the Jordanian reaction. It was in fact too cynical a view. It is now quite evident that Israel was not happy about the risks of a Jordanian attack on the central front, while her main forces were tied up in Sinai.

On 31 May Brigadier-General Uzzi Narkiss (Central Command) was told by General Dayan: 'Don't bother the General Staff with requests for reinforcements. Grit your teeth and ask for nothing.' That was the attitude. The task was to protect Jerusalem, Tel Aviv, and the heavily populated plain area, the base of Israel's army. An offensive was not contemplated. Very soon after the first Israeli air-strike had hit Egypt Mr. Eshkol asked General Odd Bull to pass a message to King Hussein: 'We shall not initiate any action whatsoever against Jordan. However, should Jordan open hostilities, we shall react with all our might and he will have to bear the full responsibility for all the consequences.'

King Hussein was in an extremely awkward position. Public opinion positively demanded war, but he depended for air cover on the Egyptians. A military man, extremely air-minded and a good pilot, he was not the one to underrate the importance of air power. Under the circumstances his best course was to sit quiet and see how things went in Sinai. Such fence-sitting was foreign to his open and honourable character, and in any case he had given command of his forces to an Egyptian, General Abdul Munim Riad — one wonders *en passant* what the Jordanian generals thought of that arrangement.

Without air cover the Jordanians had little chance of survival let alone success. Could they have done better?

Let us say at the outset that nobody, least of all the Israelis, has complained of the bravery of their troops. At the old Palestine Police School, just north of Jerusalem, 106 of the garrison of 200 were killed before the place fell to Colonel Mordechai Goor's paratroops. The question is, could they have planned better? The answer must surely be that if they were going to get involved at all — which was obviously a mistake — they could do much more damage by launching a vigorous offensive, than by sitting in their defensive positions, harassing the Jewish part of Jerusalem, Tel Aviv and Ramat David with shell-fire, and, once their air force had been shot out of the sky, being bombed with napalm.

Even when the Egyptian Air Force had been destroyed the Jordanians had one advantage. The Israelis were bound to respect the Holy Places and would be reluctant to use their air power against troops in their own country for fear of killing Jewish nationals. At Stalingrad the Russians, outnumbered in the air by the *Luftwaffe*, found that their best course was to get to close quarters. Short of doing nothing at all, the best course open to the Jordanians was a vigorous thrust either into the Jewish part of Jerusalem or towards Tel Aviv. They were probably too weak to contemplate both. There is little evidence that General Riad made much of an effort along these lines.

Although captured Jordanian Operations Orders have been published by the Israelis these envisaged no more than raids, which, though planned, had not been carried out. A study of these orders, translations of which were published one supposes as anti-Jordanian propaganda[71], is not without interest. One was captured in the H.Q. of the Hashemite Brigade near Ramallah. It seems that similar Top Secret orders were found in the safes of all six[72] Jordanian brigades stationed on the West Bank. These orders were to be kept at Brigade H.Q.s and were only to be issued to battalions on orders from H.Q. West Bank.

In each case the force detailed was an infantry battalion with artillery and engineers under command.

---

[71] I am grateful to Brigadier Z. Zamir who kindly sent me a copy of 'Jordanian Operational Orders For The Destruction Of Israeli Settlements And Killing All Persons In Them'. June 1967.

[72] In Glubb Pasha's day the garrison of the West Bank was much smaller. Before the raid on Qibya (1953), where the Israelis massacred the villagers and blew up the houses, there was only one brigade. Thereafter (1953–1956) there were two, the southern with its H.Q. near the Jerusalem-Ramallah road, and the northern with its H.Q. just east of Nablus. The increase to six brigades would seem to indicate mounting tension between Israel and Jordan since 1956.

The targets were frontier settlements, in one case Sha'alabim Settlement[73] in the Latrun salient and in another Motza Colony in the Jerusalem Hills. The orders for the latter were dated 7 June 1966 and for the former April 1967.

The plans for the raid on Motza Colony were based, it would seem, on fairly accurate information. The inhabitants were estimated at about 800 persons. The colony was surrounded by slit-trenches and barbed wire. The houses were of concrete. Five posts were manned at night. From the time when an alarm was raised it took the inhabitants from five to seven minutes to man their positions.

Camps from which reinforcements might come were listed with apparent accuracy:

Castel Camp. Infantry company with support detachments.
Shneller Camp. 6th Brigade Reconnaissance Company.
Abu Gosh Camp. Border Police Company.

Lastly, and with remarkable realism, it was conceded that the enemy had air superiority.

The aim of the operation was stated with brutal frankness. 'The intention of H.Q. Western Front is to carry out a raid on MOTZA Colony, to destroy it and to kill all its inhabitants.' A generation that has supped full of horrors can still sometimes be shocked by the savagery of war on the frontiers of Israel. Suffice it to say that these reprisal raids planned by the Jordanians imitated with flattering accuracy the pattern of those carried out by the Israelis — Qibya, Qalqilya and Samu.

Carry the story back to 1948 and in the matter of atrocities you may find neither side spotless. If the Stern Gang was guilty of the massacre at Dir Yassin, it was Arabs that burnt the

---

[73] This task was allotted to the Hashemite Brigade.

convoy of doctors and nurses in Sheikh Jarrah a few days later. Nor have such exploits been confined to Palestine. Let he that is guiltless throw the first stone. But this is not quite the point. No sensible commander will encourage his men to kill women and children, for to do so is as cowardly as it is shameful. And who wants to command cowards?

The task of taking Motza was assigned to the reserve battalion of the Imam Aly Ben Abi Taleb Brigade, with the second battery of the First Field Artillery Regiment and a platoon of engineers in direct support. It was to be a night raid. An infantry company (less one platoon) with support weapons — mortars and heavy machineguns — was to form a firm base, while another company, plus one platoon and the engineers was to break in and destroy the colony. Taking a platoon as about 35 men the company inside the colony would be considerably outnumbered by the inhabitants, however, surprise, darkness and the presence of women, children and the aged would offset any numerical advantage on the side of the Israelis. Other parties were to establish roadblocks.

The rest of the plan, which is given in all the detail beloved of staff officers, is of little interest to the general reader. Suffice it to say that having cut the required number of throats the raiders were to depart by the track from Sheikh Abd el Aziz to Bet Sorik, and at the assembly point they were to get in their vehicles and drive back to their base at Betunya.

The orders were signed by one Ahmed Shehada el Huarta, whose brigade seems to have consisted of Zeid Ben Hartha/33 Battalion, Abd el Rahman el Ghafeqi/35 Battalion, Issamu Ben Zeid Battalion, with the 1st Field Arty. Regt, in support.

Quite apart from the somewhat heavy-handed aim, the connoisseur of night operations and of commando raids might criticise the whole plan as being rather ponderous and overelaborate. One point of detail is that no provision was made for illuminating the target, though this can be of prime importance in a night attack.

It is true the Jordanians occupied Government House from which they permitted themselves to be ejected at a cost to the Israelis of only eight killed. There was a report by Amman Radio (1245 on 5 June) that Mount Scopus had been occupied, which is evidence that its importance was appreciated, but not that it was ever firmly in Jordanian hands. In short, General Riad provoked the Israelis by heavy firing, surrendered the initiative to his enemy, and, having seen the Jordanian Army shattered, departed for his native Egypt. It was not a brilliant contribution.

Of the commanders fighting the Jordanians Generals Narkiss (Central Command) and Elazar (Northern Command) were both old Palmach men. The latter had been Director of Armour. Colonel Mordechai Goor (paratroop brigade) represents the younger generation. Indeed he told me when in October 1966 I visited the Israeli Command and General Staff School, which he then commanded, that he had only joined the I.D.F. because of his indignation at the Jerusalem Incident of 1954[74]. If that is so the 9th Regiment of the Arab Legion gave the I.D.F. an outstanding officer, and the man who took the Old City.

General Narkiss appears to have been something of a fire-eater. He felt that the commanders in Sinai were going to have all the fighting. Though he had been preparing to absorb an

---

[74] The author was commanding the Arab Legion in Jerusalem at that time and has described what he believed took place in *Bedouin Command*. The Israeli and Jordanian versions of what took place do not coincide. That need cause nobody any surprise.

attack he told Rabin early on the 5th (0933) that he was ready to take Latrun, Government House and Abdul Aziz.

During the morning he pressed Rabin, Barlev (Deputy Chief of Staff) and Dayan himself for permission to advance and ordered his armoured brigade (Colonel Uri Ben-Ari) to move up from Ramleh to its prearranged positions near Jerusalem. As late as 1300 Dayan merely told him that if Mount Scopus was in danger he could go. Even so the attitude of the Israeli High Command was hardening. Two factors must have influenced them. The first was their success in the air battle with Egypt. The second was that Tal's progress meant that airborne action against El Arish was no longer required, and Colonel Goor's brigade of paratroopers was, therefore, available for action at Jerusalem. Revenge was in the air. That morning (0927) King Hussein had been heard on Amman radio: 'The hour of revenge has come...' To Rabin, Narkiss and Ben-Ari, all three born in Jerusalem and all three defeated there in 1948, it was the same thing.[75]

Meanwhile the Jordanian artillery went on pounding away. An Israeli correspondent describes that morning: 'Entire Jewish Jerusalem became a battlefield, the population vanished into the shelters, supplies were difficult to obtain and carry home, one had to hug the walls to get to the nearest grocery, there were hundreds of wounded and an undisclosed number of killed. The Hebrew University, the Hadassah Hospital, the Israel Museum, the President's residence and many other public buildings suffered direct hits together with hundreds of other private houses.

'Arab posts on the Old City walls opened mortar and machine gun fire on the city from well prepared positions. Even the Brigade Command Post in the city was hit and had to

---

[75] Cf. Churchill, pp. 128 & 130.

be moved elsewhere. Reports began to flow in that Jordanian forces had occupied the hilltop High Commissioner's Palace in the southern sector. The residence served as H.Q. of the U.N. Truce Supervision Organization under General Odd Bull. Israeli forces reacted quickly and this was the beginning of the battle for Jerusalem.

'"We broke into the U.N. with armour and the Legion began retreating into the garden and then further to the rear", one of the officers related. "We met General Bull inside the Palace." There were polite exchanges of "good morning" and the U.N. force agreed not to move. The situation was most delicate since the place had to be flushed. Women and children were in their rooms. Orders were given to evacuate them. They behaved calmly even under fire. General Bull was the last to leave. "You were quicker than they were," he told the Israeli soldiers.

'Then came the turn of the "Sausage Position", a range of fortifications stretching from the U.N. Headquarters and manned by two Jordanian companies. After that it was the village of Sur Bahar, and the "Bell" position[76] which concluded the first day's fighting. Throughout resistance was fierce, but the Israelis had broadened their front to the south and had created an improved defence line for the city.'

---

[76] This fighting ended about 1550 on the 5th.

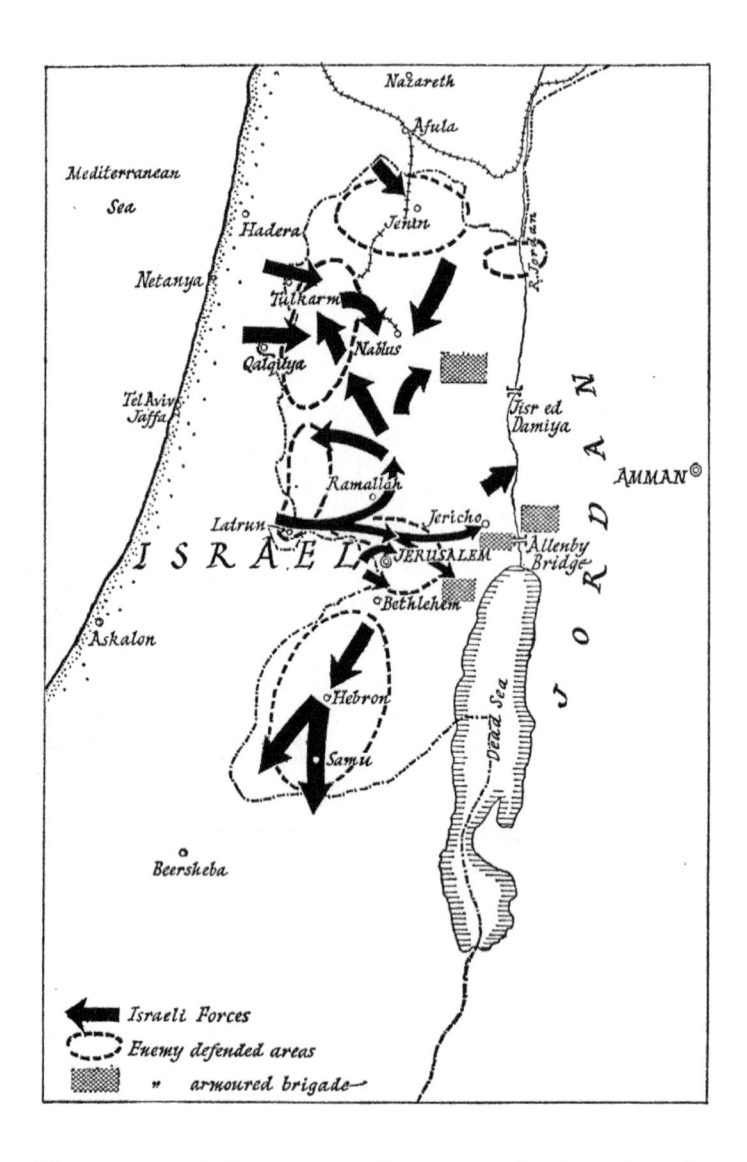

The capture of Government House was the first sign of a pincers movement enveloping the Old City. The next was the advance of the armoured brigade, which entered Jordan by 1730 and took Abdul Aziz Hill, Radar[77] and Bet Iksa.

Meanwhile (1715) the Israeli Air Force, already able to turn to offensive air support of the ground forces — the third phase of air operations in a limited war situation — had been ordered to deal with the 60th Jordanian Armoured Brigade.

The next move was to be Goor's thrust to join up Mount Scopus, for the Old City of Jerusalem, with its solid, lofty, golden walls, dating back to the days of Suleiman the Magnificent lies in a bowl surrounded by hills, the most dominant being Mount Scopus of which the Mount of Olives forms part.

The task of storming a fortified built-up area, was a tough one, but the paratroopers received their orders with enthusiasm.

Goor's plan was to make a night attack, two battalions up, with artillery and tank support.

The Israelis opened up at 0220 on the 6th, then one battalion advanced on Sheikh Jarrah and the other against the Police School. Street-fighting is difficult enough at any time, but by night few generals would even attempt it. But the Israelis are not the men to stick to 'the book'. Goor describes the attack:

'This was fighting of a sort I had never experienced. The men had to break through at least five fences before they reached the emplacements. They passed the first line of positions and entered the trenches. The fighting was going on

---

[77] An important position near Nebi Samwil, which was stormed in 1943 by a detachment of the 1st Regiment Arab Legion under Salameh Etayek. He was shot in the leg and won the Jordanian Gallantry Medal. He was afterwards my second-in-command in the 9th Regiment. In 1956 he supported the *putsch* against Glubb Pasha by Major-General Ali Nawar. I was informed last year that he has since died.

in the trenches, in the houses, on the roofs, in the cellars, anywhere and everywhere. We passed from one position to another and saw the marks left by our artillery which had been outstandingly effective. Some of the concrete bunkers had received direct hits and been destroyed.' This phase of the fighting went on for nearly five hours.

Goor describes the capture of a concealed bunker armed with two heavy machine-guns, which they had not spotted on the air photographs, indeed, an Israeli officer actually got on top of it before he realized that it was there. An Israeli soldier, exposing himself fearlessly, dropped a grenade into the position, but the shooting did not cease. Another man threw in three explosive charges and the bunker blew up. Three of its occupants were killed, but the two survivors went on firing, until another grenade put an end to their resistance.

Casualties were heavy on both sides. The paratroop battalion attacking the Police School, where the Arab Legion 'fought like hell', lost 50 of its 500 men, killed.

The Israelis gave fire support by 120mm mortars and artillery in position near Castel. Two searchlights lit up the area from the roof of the Histadrut (Federation of Labour) building. The Israeli Air Force were actually able to make air-strikes on the Police School and other targets by night!

In the vicinity of the American Colony the Jordanians did not give up the struggle easily.

Retreating Jordanians took cover in buildings, sometimes occupying houses which the Israelis had already passed, and firing into their rear. The attackers were often compelled to clear the same house twice. At dawn a tank battalion was sent in to support the Israeli infantry and cleared their main axis of advance as far as the Rockefeller Museum.

The tower of this solid earthquake-proof building had served as an Arab Legion Observation Post in 1948.

The Arab Legion still held the Old City and the paratroopers' attack had rather lost its momentum. Even so the armoured brigade and the paratroopers made contact at French Hill, an important tactical position NW of Mount Scopus, at midday on 6 June. There was indecisive fighting during the rest of the day. Then at 0500 on 7 June Barlev telephoned: 'We are already being pressed for a cease-fire. We are at the Canal. The Egyptians have been carved up — don't let the Old City remain an enclave.'[78] At 0830 the paratroops went into action once more. Colonel Goor gives a vivid and illuminating account of the assault.

He had no illusions as to the difficulty of his task, and was compelled to adopt tactics which in the ordinary way would be considered too hazardous. He had three regiments. One was to drive straight uphill from Mount Scopus to the Augusta Viktoria Hospital on the summit of the Mount of Olives. Another was to make 'a daylight frontal attack with the Old City wall behind it'. This unit was to advance through a built-up area, presumably the houses in the neighbourhood of the Rockefeller Museum. Goor does not tell us specifically what its objective was, but it seems it was intended to support the thrust at the Augusta Viktoria. The third regiment, advancing from the Musrara Quarter near Herod's Gate (alias the Damascus Gate), was to push on, regardless of fire from the Old City Wall, and break into the Temple area via St. Stephen's Gate, which is the eastern end of the Via Dolorosa.

The situation was far from clear as Goor explained:

'Not knowing for sure what the enemy position was, we decided to disregard our lack of information and proceed

---

[78] Churchill, p. 139.

according to plan. We therefore brought in the Air Force at 0830 hours. Although the Mount Scopus regiment asked for another 15 minutes, I could not let them have it, and gave orders to attack at once. I instructed our tanks to start moving up and see where contact was being effected with the enemy, and to determine the battle plan accordingly. We laid down a heavy artillery cover. Our tanks advanced firing in every direction, and, after them, I sent a mechanized unit with recoilless guns. Now everything broke loose. We jumped into the command half-track and pushed forward, giving the Mount Scopus regiment its orders to advance at top speed and the second regiment to start its frontal attack. We knew there were tanks further on, so we turned our column along the ridge and swept it with heavy fire. This same thrust brought us to the square facing the Old City. The Temple Mount was before us, with its gold and silver cupolas, and all the New City beyond.

'At this point, I ordered my brigade to attack the Old City. The plan called for a tank advance along the road to the gate, three infantry regiments were also ordered to move as far forward as possible — and whoever came first, well, that would be his luck.

'We now started shelling the Moslem quarter of the Old City which borders upon the wall and might have prevented our forces from breaking through Herod's Gate. The shelling lasted 10 minutes and was highly effective. All our tanks opened fire, as did our recoilless guns; we swept the whole wall and not a shot was directed at, or hit, the Holy Places. The breakthrough area underwent concentrated fire: all the wall shook and some stones were loosened — but all the firing was to the right of St. Stephen's Gate.

'Seeing the tanks advancing towards the wall, we got into our half-track and went on to catch up with them, while ordering them to go faster. The infantry was ordered to keep up with the tanks. For a moment, I stopped the artillery fire but after our tanks had spotted the enemy positions, we renewed our firing and continued our advance up to the bridge beneath St. Stephen's Gate. There the tanks found it more difficult to manoeuvre, but it was by this time impossible to check our impetus.

'I told my driver, Ben Tsur, a bearded fellow weighing some 15 stone, to speed on ahead. We passed the tanks and saw the Gate before us with a car burning outside it. There wasn't a lot of room, but I told him to drive on and so we passed the burning car and saw the Gate half-open in front. Regardless of the danger that somebody might drop grenades into our halftrack from above, he pushed on and flung the door aside, crunched over the fallen stones, passed by a dazed Arab soldier, turned left and came to another gate. Here, a motorcycle blocked the way but, despite the danger of a booby-trap, my driver drove right over it and we reached the Temple Mount. Here there was no more firing, for it is a Holy Place. Our tanks could not get there but the infantry regiments did.'

At this point the Governor came to Goor and surrendered the City. There was still some mopping-up to be done, but the Old City was back in Israeli hands. General Dayan came to the Western Wall of the Temple destroyed in the days of Titus (A.D.70) and said: 'We have returned to our holiest of holy places, never to be parted from it again.' General Golen sounded the shofar ...

Its sound echoed round the Jewish World, bringing tears of joy, and stiffening the resolve that Israel shall live.

The fighting elsewhere in Jordan is overshadowed by the epic storming of Jerusalem. Yet from a technical point of view it is not without interest. Ben-Ari took Ramallah in the dark (6 June) 'with a battalion of tanks, shooting on all sides. We crossed and recrossed the city several times and it slowly fell silent. There was some resistance from bazookas, etc., but within three-quarters of an hour the town was silent. We cleared out of it that night and took up positions to the north and to the south. By morning there was no resistance and the town was mopped up.' The same technique was later successful at Jericho (7 June).

In the north, as General Elazar put it: 'The Jordanians failed to recognize our main effort'. They were not unnaturally sensitive to the possibility of a thrust down the Jordan Valley from Beisan and it was in fact a feint from this direction that induced the Jordanians to split their 40th Armoured Brigade (88 Patton tanks) which was in reserve near the Jisr[79] ed Damia. With their 30 tanks at Jenin it is probable that they slightly outnumbered Elazar's armour.

The force that took Nablus entered Jordan not at Tulkarm but at Jenin. The valley that leads from Tulkarm to Nablus is narrow and lends itself to defence and delaying tactics. The British officers of the Arab Legion clearly appreciated the danger of a thrust via Jenin and the so-called Tubas Gap at the Jordanian L. of C. from Nablus to the Jisr ed Damia, and a defensive position covering this route had been reconnoitred and to some extent constructed as early as 1955. The Jordanians never seemed particularly impressed by these preparations, presumably because they hoped — rather unrealistically — to defend every single frontier village and so prevent any serious penetration of their territory. But as it

---

[79] Bridge.

turned out the defenders of Nablus were taken by surprise by an Israeli force entering the town from the East, having advanced via Jenin and Tubas. The inhabitants applauded the Israelis under the impression that they could only be Iraqis.

It is tempting to think that had the Jordanians concentrated their armour at Jenin and thrust into the Plain of Esdraelon, they might have done some good. But this is to forget that from an early hour on the 5th they were subjected to frequent air strikes, which hampered the movements of fighting troops and their first-line transports. Many Jordanian tanks ran out of fuel, and over 40 were captured undamaged. Another 45 were destroyed. It is estimated that the two Jordanian brigades in the north (25th Infantry and 40th Armoured) suffered 3,000 casualties. They were virtually destroyed.

A nation determined to continue the struggle even though its army has been defeated in the field generally resorts to guerrilla warfare. In the Peninsular War the Spaniards met with disaster after disaster when they tried to meet the French in pitched battle. One recalls the delightful occasion when Don Gregorio de la Cuesta was ridden over by his own bodyguard in its haste to quit the field — surely a unique experience? Yet these same Spaniards who made such a miserable showing in open fight, proved immensely formidable as guerrilleros. Mina, El Empecinado and Don Julian Sanchez contributed as much and more to the outcome as Castaños, Blake or La Romaña. In 1870, after Sedan, the French, with their *francs-tireurs* looked for a time as if they meant to resort to the same tactics. The military history of this century is full of examples of partisan warfare, from T. E. Lawrence onwards, and it is significant that the Arabs have shown a certain talent for this style of fighting. The exploits of the Sherifian Army in 1915–1918, of Haj Amin Husseini's adherents in Palestine 1936–1939, and the more recent successes of the Algerians may be cited to support this view. But it would be misleading to make too much of these instances. Raiding of the sort beloved of Auda Abu Tayi could not survive the advent of plane and tank, of helicopter and armoured car. An uprising such as that of the Mufti of Jerusalem against the British mandatory government is scarcely likely in the Israel of today. The Israeli Government has advantages, which the British did not possess. Quite apart from modern weaponry — notably the helicopter — they have in their forces innumerable Arabic speaking soldiers, an inestimable advantage in internal security work of this kind. Moreover the Israelis are prepared to be much tougher in suppressing guerrilla warfare than the British were. The British had perhaps a certain sympathy for the Arabs. The Israelis, with more at stake, and with, it must be said, a more ruthless outlook, would not hesitate to resort to strong-arm methods — hostages, fines, demolished houses and so forth. They would, moreover, hound the rebels by day and night. The British soldier — at any rate in peacetime — prefers to go to bed at night, which is, oddly enough, just the time when the partisan is most active. If this were not so how could Grivas have survived in Cyprus? But that is another story.

It is not absolutely beyond the bounds of possibility that there should be guerrilla activity in the territory taken from Jordan, but it seems unlikely that it will amount to much. The Jordanian soldier, trained for so long on rather formal British lines is not particularly likely to abandon the methods of regular warfare — 'high port in the moonlight'; 'two[80] up and bags of smoke' and all the cries so dear to our contemporaries. Once long ago I suggested to my superiors in the Arab Legion that the answer to the growing power of the Israeli Air Force

---

[80] Platoons.

might be a Commando trained, like the S.A.S. of the Second World War, to destroy aircraft on the ground. The idea was but coldly received by the pundits. Yet I am convinced that the Bedouin soldier, with his undoubted talent for finding his way about, would be very good indeed for work of this sort. Indeed I believe my point has been proved by no less an authority than General Dayan himself. On the night 10/11 October, 1956, about six months after Glubb Pasha and his British officers were dismissed from the Arab Legion, Israeli paratroops commanded by such fire-eaters as Arik Sharon and Mordechai Goor, carried out a reprisal raid on Qalqilya and blew up the Police Station. One hesitates to criticise the dispositions of such experienced raiders, but in my view they sent their road-blocking group too far into Jordan: six miles. It chanced that the 9th Regiment of the Arab Legion, which I had commanded until the previous March, was encamped at Azun. Two companies in 15 trucks set out for Qalqilya, were ambushed, lost the first four vehicles, and went back. The Israelis moved their ambush and about an hour later shot up another relief convoy, hitting two vehicles. So far from being dismayed by their previous losses the Jordanians now put into practice their previous training. Up to midnight, when it was ordered to withdraw, the Israeli blocking unit had suffered no casualties. But as soon as they began to withdraw they came under heavy fire. 'The Legion troops who had not managed to advance by vehicle had dismounted and taken up positions in the rear of our unit, so that our men who had blocked the road against the Jordanian reinforcements now found their own route back to Israel blocked. The Jordanians quickly went over to the attack, and in a short time out of our fifty-four men, there were eleven wounded and one killed.'[81] Not bad shooting

---

[81] Diary of The Sinai Campaign, p. 49.

in the dark. A hard fight followed and eventually an Israeli convoy broke through in half-tracks to relieve the beleaguered paratroops, but it was a desperate affair.

Dayan wrote in his diary: 'During the last two years, paratroop units have on numerous occasions gone out on actions across the border, and only once was one of their wounded left behind in enemy territory. Now there was an entire unit, more than fifty men, in desperate straits, their ammunition spent, their officers out of action, cut off, and surrounded by the Legion's Bedouin troops.'[82] The Israelis lost 18 killed, including eight officers and more than 50 wounded, 14 being officers. The Arab losses are not known though the Israelis put them at 'about a hundred killed'.[83]

It is possible, as so often in war, to fault the tactics of either side. That, however, is not the point. The lesson of the Qalqilya raid is that the Bedouin soldier, with training, is capable of attaining a standard of efficiency in the conduct of night operations sufficient to fit him for commando operations of the most exacting sort. This is not, however, to say that the so-called 'commandos', the men of El-Fatah, or the vaunted Egyptian *fedayeen* are likely to give the Israelis much trouble either in the Gaza strip or on the Golan Heights.

In the teeth of superior numbers and overwhelming air superiority the Jordan Army had done its best. If its manoeuvres were not distinguished by any tactical brilliance their Egyptian general must bear the responsibility.

The Jews, especially in Jerusalem, had fought like men inspired. Martin Bennett, a reservist aged 22, flew out from London and within 10 hours was in action with the Paratroop's

---

[82] Dayan, p. 49.
[83] Dayan, p. 43.

Scout Regiment. In the fierce hand-to-hand fighting for the old City his unit lost 60 killed.[84] Colonel Goor said:

'They were the pick of the best, it is difficult to evaluate them properly, those shopkeepers, clerks and farmers. Many were wounded a number of times. Some were over age, but when they mounted the steps to the temple square they were the happiest men in the world, even though some of them were barely alive.'

The Arabs who can remove them *may* have been born. They have not yet been trained.

---

[84] BBC, 13 June 1967.

CHAPTER IX: NOISES OFF

A plague o' both your houses.
                Mercutio. Romeo and Juliet, *Act III, Scene I.*

At 3 a.m. Abba Eban telephoned Gideon Rafael, Israeli ambassador to the United Nations, and told him that war had broken out. He got his word in first. At 9.30 Hans Tabor (Danish Ambassador) informed the 1347th meeting of the Security Council:

'At 3:10 this morning, the permanent representative of Israel to the United Nations informed me officially, in my capacity as president of the council, as follows: I have just received reports that Egyptian land and air forces have moved against Israel and Israel forces are now engaged in repelling the Egyptian forces.'

Twenty minutes later Mohamed Awad el Kony (U.A.R.) telephoned Tabor:

'Israel has committed a treacherous premeditated aggression against the United Arab Republic this morning.'

Israel had perhaps scored a point, but in truth it is one of purely academic interest. Beyond question she had started the battle. But it is equally certain that Nasser had begun the campaign when he occupied Sharm-el-Sheikh. The war itself had started in 1948. An armistice is not a peace.

At 4:30 a.m. Mr. Walt Whitman Rustow woke Mr. Johnson by telephone and informed him that war had broken out. It is reported that the latter was not surprised. Nor indeed does he seem to have been unduly disturbed as to the fate of Israel. It seems that the Joint Chiefs of Staff had provided him with an accurate appreciation of the possibilities, whichever side struck first.

If Mr. Johnson took these events with an admirable *sang-froid* the same cannot be said of the rest of the world. Everywhere people speculated as to whether once more the Human Race had succeeded in getting itself to the brink of war. Soldiers of a generation too young to have seen World War Two or Korea longed for the chance to distinguish themselves. Officer cadets conjured up visions of immediate commissions. Lesser mortals wondered whether their statesmen would manage to bring about an early cease-fire.

The U.S.S.R. was swift with a statement, which like that of 23 May, gave the Arabs somewhat vague and therefore misleading indications of Soviet support:

'On 5th June, 1967, Israel started military operations against the United Arab Republic, thus committing aggression.... Thus a military conflict has flared up in the Middle East because of the adventurism of the rulers of one country, Israel, which has been encouraged by covert and overt actions of certain imperialist circles.' Israel, the Russians demanded, must 'stop immediately and unconditionally' military operations against the Arab States, and, while expressing the hope that the great Powers and U.N.O. would do everything to restore peace, the U.S.S.R. reserved the right 'to take all steps that may be necessitated by the situation'. Moscow Radio's Arabic Service declared that 'The oil tycoons in the West have always been and still are the main architects of all the plots and intrigues against the progressive Arab States, especially the U.A.R. and Syria'.

The Vatican lost no time in appealing to both sides to respect the shrines and monuments of the Holy Land. In a message to U Thant the Pope said: 'In the name of Christianity we voice the fervent hope that in the unfortunate eventuality — which we firmly trust will never occur — that the situation may worsen, Jerusalem may, because of its peculiar sacred and holy character, be declared an open and inviolable city.'

Algeria declared war on Israel following what she was pleased to describe as 'Zionist aggression'. Predictably, there were attacks on the British Council and the U.S. Consulate.

King Hassan of Morocco issued orders for the despatch of army units, some of which left for the front.

President Bourguiba of Tunisia sent messages of support to President Nasser and other Arab leaders. The mobs went into action against the British and American embassies in Tunis.

The Emperor Haile Selassie of Ethiopia, the Lion of Judah, issued a statement saying that in the event of the Security Council failing to put a stop to the Middle East conflict, an emergency session of the General Assembly would have to be summoned. In appealing to all countries to help to bring about a cease-fire, he described the situation as potentially dangerous to all mankind.

Guinea broke off diplomatic relations with Israel, 'an instrument of international imperialism'. The Israeli Ambassador and a number of technicians working in the country were expelled.

President Osman of Somalia, on hearing of Israel's 'unprovoked aggression', once more assured the Arab leaders of his full support, and asked the Shah of Persia to deny Israel oil.

President Makarios sent Nasser a message of Cypriot solidarity.

The Belgian Foreign Secretary, Monsieur Harmel, appealing to members of the Security Council to work for a peaceful settlement, said that no solution could be accepted which did not recognize the right to existence of all the states concerned, and the freedom of navigation in international waters.

In Colombia both U.A.R. and Israeli Ambassadors claimed that Colombians had volunteered to fight for their cause.

Arabs rioted in Sofia, demonstrating outside the British, American and Israeli missions, breaking windows, and setting fire to cars. The Bulgarian Police restored order ...

France suspended arms deliveries to both contestants, a move which meant much more to Israel than the Arabs, since the Israeli Air Force was entirely equipped with French planes. President de Gaulle cancelled an official visit to Poland due to start on 6 June.

In Britain a Gallup Poll (29 May–4 June) had asked the question: 'Who are your sympathies with in the Middle East dispute, Israel or Egypt and other Arab countries?' The answer was: Israel 46%; Egypt 4%; Neither 50%.

Mr. George Brown, the Foreign Secretary in Mr. Harold Wilson's (Socialist) Government, told a crowded House that Britain's concern must be 'not to take sides', and her aim 'to bring about an early and general cease-fire'. Sir Alec Douglas-Home, his Conservative 'shadow', concurred, while wondering if the cease-fire resolution might not be more effective if it embodied some form of U.N. peace-keeping machinery to separate the combatants.

To quote *The Economist* (10 June 1967): 'The Middle East war was a one-day disaster for the European stock-markets. On Monday morning, most shares were marked down all over Europe. There was some real selling of oil shares everywhere; Swiss-based investors, with their usually exquisitely bad sense of timing, sold heavily — indeed in Frankfurt, the banks, acting for these investors, sold short. In Paris falls reached 7% in oil shares, and in Milan the market fall was 3%. In London it was under 2%, and most of that occurred in the first hour of trading.'

In New York the war sent brokers on an 'emotional binge'. Share prices went into 'their broadest, deepest dive' since October 1966, and the Dow-Jones industrial average dropped 15.54 points. 'War has become an exceedingly dirty word on Wall Street these days.'

While these are a sample of the reactions in the seats of the mighty, more ordinary folk were responding as their individual natures, emotions and backgrounds dictated.

In London, Topol, bearded star of a successful Jewish musical, 'Fiddler on the Roof', quit Her Majesty's Theatre to volunteer to go and entertain the troops. Lt. Colonel Albeck, a student at the Staff College, Camberley, took 10 days' leave and arrived in Jerusalem in time to take over a battalion whose commander had fallen.

The British Zionist Federation called a rally at the Royal Albert Hall, and 9,000 people turned up to hear speeches by the Chief Rabbi, Dr. Immanuel Jakobovitz, and representatives of the three main parties. There was strong criticism of the British government's policy of 'sitting on the fence'. Mr. Donald Silk (chairman of the Federation) said he intended to volunteer for service of any kind in Israel, and appealed for volunteers between the ages of 18 and 40.

Mr. Quintin Hogg, M.P., said he was not a Jew; 'I am here in a sense to show that there still can be honour in public life.'

In several Arab countries the outbreak of hostilities sparked off a wave of antisemitism. In Egypt about 350 Jews were detained and the Chief Rabbis of Cairo and Alexandria are said to have been put under house arrest. Fifty-four of those arrested had Italian passports. When they reached Naples the following Sunday, they described how they had been arrested on the 5th, taken from homes, shops and offices, beaten, and left for long periods without food or water. Seven were children who had become separated from their parents.

In Tripoli things were much worse. Sixteen Jews were thrown from roofs or balconies, and the driver of an American school bus was burned to death in his cab by the mob.

In Lebanon the government had the sense to seal off the 6,000 inhabitants of the Jewish quarter with troops and armoured cars.

In the Crater area of Aden the elderly Mr. Mayer Awadh Shao was beaten to death and the synagogue set on fire. Terrorists shot at the firemen, but fortunately proved poor marksmen.

Algeria continued to show herself the most active of Nasser's supporters. The arrival of Algerian MiGs in the U.A.R. on the 7th was tangible proof of her solidarity with the other Arab countries. Following the Security Council's call for a cease-fire the Foreign Minister, Bouteflika, arrived for talks with Nasser. The cease-fire was rejected.

Morocco was less belligerent, though at Casablanca tug crews refused to work British and American ships and the strike spread to Tangier. President Bourguiba of Tunisia sent a special envoy to Cairo for talks with President Nasser, their first direct contact since diplomatic relations had been severed over the Palestine question in October 1966. Nevertheless the despatch of troops was postponed.

The Government of Burundi pledged full and unconditional support for the U.A.R. in its fight against Israel and the 'imperialist powers hiding behind them'. A Bujumbura radio talk confirmed that this summed up the views of the whole Burundi people. Rather more helpfully President Hamani Diori of Niger, President of O.C.A.M., stated that the members of that organization approved without reservation the Security Council resolution, and reaffirmed their desire to do everything possible to make it effective.

In the Somali Republic over 1,000 youths volunteered to fight alongside the Arabs. In Hargeisa a crowd demonstrated against alleged British and American intervention in the War. The Defence Minister met the U.A.R. ambassador and his Military Attaché and discussed sending troops. The Boy Scouts announced their willingness to throw themselves into the struggle, and, perhaps somewhat more practically, the Somali Women's Association said it would despatch a Red Crescent unit to the theatre of war.

President Kaunda appealed to the great powers not to get involved in the hostilities and to cease the supply of arms. Zambia believed that the recommendation of the Security Council was a step in the right direction.

The French Government also welcomed the Security Council's cease-fire decision, and advocated a four power examination of the fundamental problems affecting relations between Israel and her Arab neighbours. It was revealed that President de Gaulle and Mr. Kosygin had exchanged messages by the special teleprinter link. The Foreign Secretary, Monsieur Couve de Murville, defended France's neutral position. She would continue to advocate an international convention on the freedom of navigation in the Gulf of Aqaba so as to ensure a lasting settlement.

The Austrian Government called on all the Middle East powers to recognize their responsibility for world peace, and hoped that the Security Council, supported by the great powers, would put an end to the fighting. The conservative paper *Volksblatt* revealed sympathy for Israel which had been 'forced against its will to fight its enemies'.

The *East German Radio* commented that: 'To reject the policy of the Israeli Government and its aggression is no more anti-semitic than the attitude of the millions of Hitler's opponents in the Second World War was anti-German'.

Magalhaes Pinto, the Brazilian Foreign Minister, said that the U.N. decision to recommend an immediate cease-fire had enhanced the prestige of that organization and had increased the possibility of holding a peace conference, as proposed by Brazil. It was announced that the Brazilian U.N. contingent was being evacuated on the 7th, though a number of officers and men had reported to the Israeli Embassy as volunteers for Israel. This, according to an Army spokesman, was a breach of regulations.

In Colombia the ambassadors of the U.A.R. and Israel gave their different versions of the situation at the front. Hassan Ahmed Kamil said that all reports distributed by the international news agencies that his country might be defeated were untrue. The war was developing favourably for the U.A.R. No less than 100 volunteers had reported to his embassy. He had confidence in the Egyptian army. Avigdor Shoham on the other hand said that the U.A.R. and its allies did not know how to fight, and that the results of the battles were evidence of this.

Mauritania broke off diplomatic relations with the U.S.A., which did not suffer unduly in consequence.[85]

Diplomatic activity continued frenzied and diverse. The Arab leaders, scarcely able to credit the completeness of the destruction of their air forces, came to the conclusion that

---

[85] The reader may recall that Mauritania had severed relations with Great Britain in 1965. (Then again they may not.)

Israel must have had help from America and Britain. The clandestine *Voice of Iraqi People*, which operated from Eastern Europe, broadcast an accusation of the American and British governments for 'permitting their aircraft, men and arms to be used in supporting Israel and intercepting the Arab aircraft which destroyed the bases of aggression'.

Albania, China's ally, in step with her East European allies — for once — condemned Israel's aggression.

In the Far East editors fired off their long range salvoes. The Pekin *People's Daily* took both Russia and America for targets. In an article 'Accomplice of U.S. imperialism unmasked' it developed its own curious thesis:

'The armed attack unleashed by Israel on the Arab countries was entirely stage-managed by U.S. imperialism. But in their statement of 5 June the Soviet revisionists said not a word in condemnation of U.S. imperialism as the chief culprit of the war of aggression against the Arab countries. On the contrary, they urged "the Governments of other States", including what they called "the great powers", to "extinguish the military conflagration in the Middle East"... How absurd it is that the Soviet revisionists should have called on the incendiaries to extinguish the fire started by themselves in the Middle East! Isn't this a deliberate attempt to absolve U.S.-British imperialism from its crime?'

According to the *Korean Agency* headlines in the North Korean press declared that the Korean people would do 'everything in their power to aid the Arab people in their just struggle against U.S. imperialism and Israeli aggression'. In this case desire doubtless outran performance.

Waldeck Rochet, General Secretary of the *French Communist Party*, which had at first taken a pro-Arab line, finding that the *Federation de la Gauche* was pro-Israel, swung to advocacy of a settlement based on the State of Israel's right to exist and on the legitimate national aspirations of the Arabs.

In an editorial the Chinese *People's Daily* said that 'the frantic aggression unleashed by Israel against the Arab countries has been stage-managed single-handed by U.S. imperialism'. At the same time the 'hypocrisy' of the Russians was stressed. They were only 'false friends' of the Arabs.

This promising theme was developed along predictable lines: 'Recently, busy contacts and intensive activities have been carried on between Moscow, Washington and London. A large number of Soviet war vessels have steamed into the East Mediterranean, exchanging fraternal greetings with the warships of the U.S. Sixth Fleet... Kosygin wrote a hypocritical letter to the Israeli Premier urging him to be "cautious"... The Soviet revisionist clique is bent on stamping out the flames of the Arab people's just struggle, in collusion with U.S. and British imperialism.' It followed, as Chou En-lai did not fail to point out to President Nasser, that the Chinese were Arabia's staunchest ally — not that 'volunteers' were offered as they had been in the Lebanon crisis of 1958.

On 8 June Algeria broke off diplomatic relations with U.S.A.[86] Exports of petroleum to the U.S.A. and the U.K. were banned, their oil companies were seized and their bank accounts frozen.

The Tunisian government stated that it would send troops to 'combat Israeli aggression', but their Foreign Minister arrived in Washington, and profound regret was expressed for the damage to embassies. The demonstrators would be court-martialled!

In Ghana the *Daily Graphic* carried a shrewd leader, deploring the bitter hatred of the Arabs for Israel and Nasser's blockade

---

[86] Relations with the U.K. had been severed in 1965.

of the Gulf of Aqaba. It suggested that it was no coincidence that the Russian warships, 'probably armed with atomic weapons', had applied to Turkey to enter the Mediterranean, and wondered whether the Soviet Union did not intend to 'take advantage of the resultant confusion to gain a permanent passage into the Mediterranean Sea'.

President Houphouet-Boigny twice assured the Israeli ambassador of the Ivory Coast's total support for his country. The Israeli embassy received several offers from Ivory Coast citizens who wished to fight for Israel.

In Kenya the *Daily Nation* commented: 'the question of taking sides is largely irrelevant at this critical moment'. The *East African Standard* was more forthright. The 'aggressive initiative lay with President Nasser' and 'if World War occurs he will be mainly to blame'. In Rhodesia Salisbury Radio was equally straightforward and perceptive. The 'Russians have openly declared themselves on the side of the Arabs while the West still speaks of neutralism ... fear of a third world war, and a nuclear one at that, seems to be holding the Western powers at a safe distance from the brink while the Russians walk boldly along the edge. Britain withdrew from East of Suez by her own choice. Now the Suez is closed and the tide is lapping along the Mediterranean coast'.

Further north in Somalia an emergency meeting of the Council of Ministers decided to send a military delegation to the Arab military leaders; to recruit volunteers for the Holy War; and to call upon Somali students in Arab countries to volunteer. Permission was sought for military aircraft to fly over Ethiopian territory on their way to Egypt.

In South Africa the Foreign Minister, Dr. Muller, told the Senate that, while deploring the war, his country would pursue its policy of non-intervention. Nevertheless he pointed out that the crisis emphasized once again the importance of the sea-route round the Cape.

The Colombian Foreign Minister, while stressing his country's neutrality, favoured lifting the Egyptian blockade of the Gulf of Aqaba.

In the House of Commons Mr. Harold Wilson, the British Premier, made a declaration to a crowded House. He announced a temporary ban on shipments of arms to the war zone. He angrily denied the 'monstrous story' that British planes had intervened in the fighting. The nearest carriers were 1,000 miles away. Rejecting the blackmail of threatened cuts in oil supplies he opined that any Arab State so doing would be 'cutting off its market'. While Nasser had no right to close the Suez Canal, Mr. Wilson maintained the neutral position adopted by Mr. Brown on the previous day.

When Sir Alec Douglas-Home inquired how long the arms ban was to last, Mr. Wilson replied that the suspension would be reviewed in 24 hours. Sir Alec asked whether the U.S.S.R. had agreed to a suspension. The Premier: 'The position of Russia does need to be made known more clearly. The suspension should not be on the basis which creates unfairness on one side or the other.'

Nasser must have been disappointed by the Soviet reaction to the story of British and American aerial intervention. Russian warships were too near the U.S. Sixth Fleet for there to be any doubt in Moscow that the allegations were utterly false.

'On Tuesday all markets were firm, and the gentlemen from Switzerland helped the Frankfurt market by buying, at higher prices, the shares they had contracted to sell the day before.' In New York also 'Israel's quick victories led to an almost complete recovery'...[87]

Israel had embarked on her campaign with some misgivings. She, like the U.S.A. in their attitude to the Vietnam War, had her 'doves' and her 'hawks'. It was by no means certain that she would take the decision to attack and it may be that here the intervention of Dayan was vital. It is ironical that this great Jewish warrior's chief contribution to the campaign may have been made before a shot was fired, for it is obvious that the training of the army, its planning, and the conduct of its operations fell on the shoulders of the self-effacing Rabin.

While Weizman and Hod had complete confidence in their ability to destroy the Egyptian Air Force, men like Eshkol and Eban, less well versed in military affairs, must have had their doubts. Remembering the clamour provoked by the Suez-Sinai Campaign of 1956, they may well have felt misgivings as to the political outcome. Then the U.S.A., the U.S.S.R. and U.N.O. had combined to denounce and thwart the aims of France, Great Britain and Israel. But the factors were now altered. In 1967 the U.S.A. and the U.S.S.R., though at one in not wishing for a general war, were not agreed as to the merits of the quarrel between Israel and her neighbours. This being so it might take more than pious wishes to bring about a cease-fire, or to make Israel surrender such territories as she should overrun.

And thus it proved, for sound and fury without action are not enough. Since the superpowers are unwilling to intervene, and U.N.O. and the Arabs incapable of doing so, it follows that Israel is not likely to be talked out of her conquests a second time. To those who demanded her withdrawal it was as if she asked the question: 'What are you going to do about it?'

The answer being 'Nothing', the time was bound to come sooner or later (in about six weeks as it turned out) when this

---

[87] *The Economist.* 10 June 1967.

particular Wonder would cease to occupy the headlines and the TV screens, yielding its place to the vagaries of Chinese foreign policy, or the question of escalation in Vietnam. Israel had got away with as neat a piece of limited war as the Nuclear Age has seen.

CHAPTER X CHRONOLOGY

0745 5 June 1967: First Israeli air-strikes against Egypt. Syrian air-strike against Haifa. Syrian Air Force broken.

0730 6 June 1967: Minor Syrian attacks on She'ar Yashuv, Tel Dan and Kibbutz Dan repulsed. Heavy shelling of Israeli settlements.

7 June 1967: Shelling.

8 June 1967: Heavy air attacks on the Syrian anti-aircraft batteries and artillery.

9 June 1967: Egypt agrees to a cease-fire.

0320 9 June 1967: Syrian defensive positions pounded from the air. Israeli Air Force pounds 'the Maginot'.

1130 9 June 1967: Zero hour for the final assault.

1430 10 June 1967: Fall of Qnaitra.

1930 June 1967: Syria accepts the cease-fire.

CHAPTER X: THE SYRIAN MAGINOT

'The Jordanians were our adversaries in war, but the Syrians are our blood enemies.'

Israeli Reservist

The theatre of war was now the northern stretch of the Jordan Valley from the Sea of Tiberias to Dan. The valley is flanked by the southern range of the mountains, Lebanon, and Anti-Lebanon, which run north, parallel to the Mediterranean coast. Mount Hermon, like a great bastion of the Anti-Lebanon, looks down upon Dan and Banias and seems to survey the whole area. South of Mount Hermon the lower range of the Anti-Lebanon has been fortified along the whole frontier between Israel and Syria as far south as the gorge of the River Yarmouk, the border with Jordan. This line — 'the Syrian Maginot' — had been constructed and improved during 19 years. It is probable that both French and Russian influences were at work in its construction, for senior Syrian officers received their early training from the French, while there is good evidence of the presence of Russian officers during the fighting in June 1967. What General Beaufre called the *'curieux style sovietique'* has already been described in the account of the Sinai Campaign. The Maginot Line, where the present writer served for a month in 1940, was organized in a deep zone consisting of three lines — Ligne de Contacte; Ligne de Recueil and Ligne d'Arrêt[88], the last being very heavily fortified

---

[88] Contact, 'Recoil' and Stop lines. The first two were intended as delaying positions to give the main position time to 'get set', while

indeed. It will be recalled that these forts fell not because they were assaulted from the front, but because, being incomplete north of Sedan, they were turned. The Syrian line, about 50 miles long and ten miles deep and with its H.Q. at Qnaitra, was manned by five infantry brigades, three up and two back, supported by a mobile force of two armoured and two mechanized brigades. There was a battalion of Russian tanks under command of each brigade, and an additional 30 tanks were dug in[89].

The Syrians were liberally provided with artillery[90] with which, from time to time, the sixteen Israeli frontier *kibbutzim* in the valley were harassed.

Sitting in their lines and bombarding border settlements was one thing. A thrust across the Jordan Valley into the mountains of Galilee was quite another. The main aims of any such an offensive would be to take Safad, Nazareth and, ultimately, Haifa. Since Nazareth is the largest Arab centre in Israel the idea was politically attractive. But though the *kibbutzim* in the Jordan Valley might be looked upon as easy victims, the hills beyond must have looked singularly unattractive to men safely ensconced in a strong position. Passing through the mountains of Galilee, often mantled with conifers and olives, one is struck by their resemblance to parts of Portugal. In short they are full of Wellingtonian defensive positions. Supposing Israel to be capable of allotting two brigades to this front there seemed no likelihood of the Syrians getting much further than Safad. And in the event they contented themselves during the early days of the war with three minor perhaps feint attacks (6 June) on Kibbutz Dan, Tel Dan and She'ar Yashuv. In each case the

---

inflicting casualties on the approaching enemy.
[89] Cf. Churchill, p. 185.
[90] There were 265 guns and 200 anti-aircraft guns. (Churchill, p. 182.)

attacking force was an infantry battalion supported by a squadron of tanks.

At Kibbutz Dan, a place of some 500 inhabitants, the mobilization, a fortnight earlier, of 50 young men and women had greatly reduced the garrison. There remained 24 middle-aged men, with some boys as runners. The Syrians attacked at 7.30 a.m. and were held up in a field by the fire of four automatic rifles. A section of 2 x 8mm mortars under one Baruch Fischer, an apple specialist, brought down 150 rounds on the attackers in twenty minutes and 'chopped the enemy up'.[91] It sounds simple. In fact it was touch and go. The Syrians replied with shellfire which fell in chicken coops only fifteen yards from the mortar position. For the rest it was a matter of bombardment which kept the women and children in their shelters for four days. At Tel Katzir, east of the Sea of Tiberias and right under the noses of the Syrians, there was heavy damage to the buildings, the dining-hall being set on fire. At Kfar Hanassi the damage was mostly to the fields and orchards. The civilian casualties on the whole frontier were twenty-nine women and children.

The Syrians did manage one raid on the Haifa refinery (5 June) before their air force was crippled.

In October 1966 Syrian-based *fedayeen*[92] of the *Fatah* organization were perpetrating their raids every other night. These usually amounted to a quick excursion — often via Lebanese or Jordanian border — the laying of a mine often of British origin — and a swift retreat. It was evident that Israeli patience was nearly at breaking point, and that a reprisal raid might take place at any time.

---

[91] *Life Atlantic*. 10 June 1967.
[92] To translate this as 'commando' is really an insult to the latter!

I stayed for several days in the *kibbutz* at Kfar Hanassi, where Colonel Robert Henriques had a house. It was only about 2,000 yards from the frontier and as a former gunner officer he used to delight in inspecting and criticizing their dispositions with the aid of a telescope. I was permitted to reconnoitre the whole of the front between Dan and the Sea of Tiberias. Two points struck me in particular. One was that the boulder-strewn slopes leading up to the Syrian position were in fact 'tankable', a point which was later proved, in practical fashion, by running an exercise over similar terrain in Galilee. The other was that the Syrian positions, though hewn from the solid rock, concreted and doubtless well wired and mined, were often clearly visible to the naked eye. Experience shows that if a defensive post is visible it is vulnerable, particularly to the Centurion with its 105mm guns. In discussion the Israeli High Command appeared to be rather impressed by the strength of this Syrian position, which was after all the strongest in the Middle East, an idea that seemed to be confirmed by the fact that the reprisal raid when it came was directed against Jordan.[93]

One of the possibilities discussed was a helicopter assault in the Qnaitra area and it is interesting to note that such an attack was included in Elazar's plan.

The cease-fire sounded, but the Israelis did not hear it: nor could they be expected to heed it until there had been a showdown on the northern front. Against Syria they would fight for revenge. With sixteen *kibbutzim* blazing like torches before their eyes the soldiers needed little encouragement to tackle the Syrian 'Maginot Line'.

From the Israeli point of view the operation was not easy. In the flat wastes of the Sinai Desert it was comparatively simple to make the most effective use of air support. In the hilly

---

[93] Samu. 13 November 1966.

country south of Mount Hermon it was by no means as easy to engage targets on the ground.

The eyewitness account of Maier Asher who watched the operation from the heights above Tiberias vividly conjures up the nature of the decisive fighting on the 9th of June.

He heard 'the rumble of enormous numbers of tanks, halftracks and vehicles assembling for the assault'. Then he attended the briefing of young reservists sitting under a tree whose commander said: 'The tanks will go up first. If they succeed in climbing over the boulders, we follow. If they are stopped you advance up the hill to clear the mines. The markings should be clear, a white ribbon on the right, green torches on the left for the night. If you meet other obstacles then call the bulldozers. Any questions?' There were none. These instructions had been heard before but the attack never seemed to materialize. The Syrian shells continued to rain. The shelling from the guns up on the mountain had become a daily routine. It was non-stop for the past four days since the first gun was fired in Sinai. At times it looked as though the order to attack the Syrians would never come although they had started the 'third round'.

Asher heard 'reports from the settlements of Dan and She'ar Yashuv in the north. Two Syrian columns with tanks were descending from the plateau near the Jordan tributary of Banias and from the fort of Neheila. Dan's pillboxes spat fire but the Syrians were still advancing to within a hundred yards of the settlement's fence. The tanks were called. The planes zoomed above. Both attacks were repulsed. But "in protest" the two settlements were shelled more fiercely than ever from the mountain positions. The main casualties were seven cows wounded at She'ar Yashuv. The settlers radioed for a veterinary surgeon. Their message was misunderstood and we saw ambulances speeding towards the settlement.

'Finally the order "Forward" crackled on the speakers and earphones of tanks and half-tracks. The Syrian line was stormed and pierced at three points. Armour and infantry started climbing the steep mountains. Big boulders stood in the way of tanks and were circumvented. In the north, the villages of Kfar Szold, Dan and She'ar Yashuv were the first to be relieved of the shelling. The Syrian position of Zaura from where it came had been taken. The column then proceeded towards the sources of the Jordan… The terrain was rough, interspersed with rivulets and small lakes. The small wooden bridges which would have collapsed under the armour's weight were not even tried and the tanks were seen splashing through the water. Here the first Syrian tanks were met. I saw them pouring fire on the Israelis who answered fiercely and at a devastating speed. Half-tracks were hit. The first wounded were waiting for help biting their lips. The tanks continued to climb, blowing up each bunker which held up their advance. The infantry followed in hand-to-hand combats inside trenches and bunkers. The Syrians resisted fiercely. They exploited fully the advantage of the terrain. Planes dived in quick succession dropping heavy bombs, "but this is not Sinai", I heard a pilot say later. "Here there are no long armoured columns. Here they are split in small groups of five or six tanks entrenched or moving but always expertly camouflaged and difficult to find." Even when the noose tightened around the dreaded gun positions they continued to fire on the settlements below. A number of times the Syrian tanks tried surprise tactics but were smashed from the air.

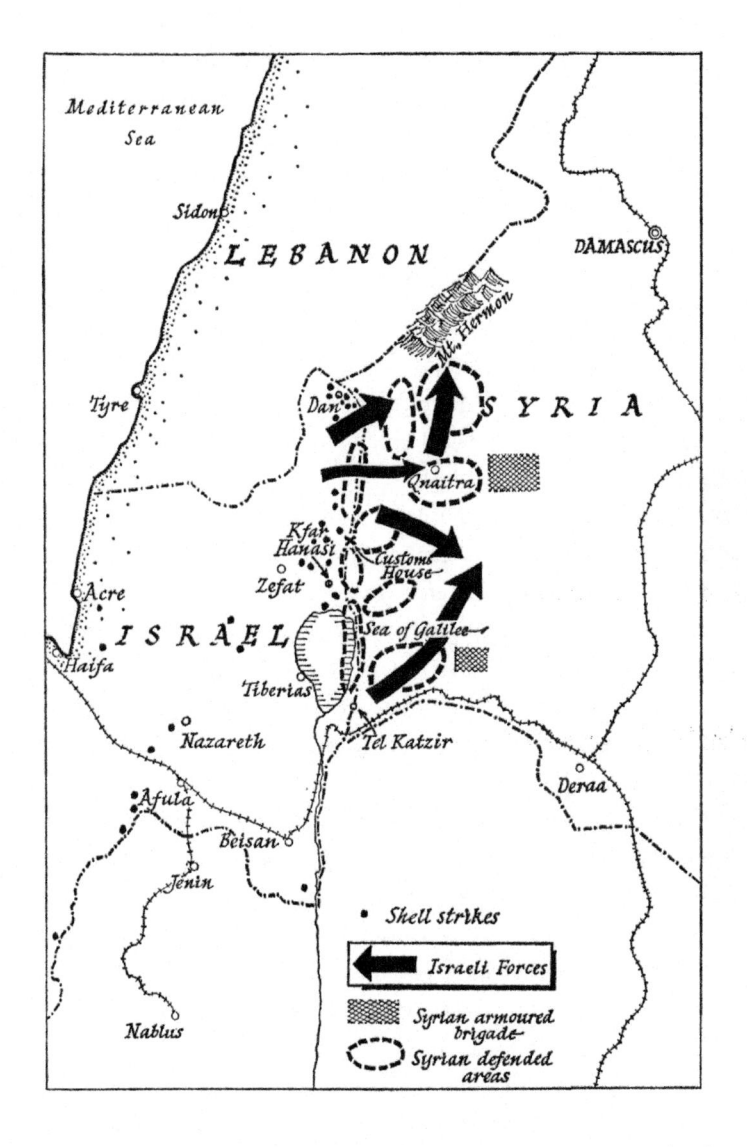

'There were many moments of tension. In one case both Israeli and Syrian armoured columns were two miles from the strategic village of Kanaba. He who entered the village first would have the advantage of protection. The control tower reported that the planes would be able to attack only in five minutes. Would the Syrian tanks cover the distance in five minutes and outdo the Israelis? They did not and never entered the village. They were destroyed by the aircraft on the outskirts.

'Then, an anti-aircraft column was reported advancing from Damascus. The guns could also be used against the tanks. All planes in the air received orders to give priority to this column advancing towards Qnaitra to relieve the besieged garrison of the H.Q. of the Syrian General Staff. The column did not arrive.

'Then, an Israeli plane was reported shot down near *kibbutz* Lehavot Habashan in the north. A helicopter was sent and landed on enemy-held territory to try and rescue the pilot. He was not found and the helicopter returned empty-handed and bullet riddled. The same helicopter later went to collect the wounded after darkness. The battle raged all night. Names of strongholds often mentioned in the news, Tel Azaziat, Darbeshiya, Djalabina, fell one after the other. The armour reached the sources of the Jordan. The old customs house on the road from Tiberias to Damascus, just over the Bridge of the Daughters of Jacob, was captured.

'Somewhere along the front a journalist managed to snatch a lift in a command jeep. Suddenly, the officer who was listening in on the Syrians' wavelength, handed the receiver to my colleague and said "Listen". He told me later he had heard coded artillery messages in Russian with the other side answering "Nye panimayu," — I cannot understand. The fact that Russians directed the Syrian artillery fire was never officially confirmed in Israel, but in one position the Israelis found a collection of Balzac in Russian translation, hardly reading for a Syrian soldier.

'On the southern sector, overlooking the Lake, the storming of the Syrian fortifications would have been even more difficult because of the almost vertical climb. A frontal attack on Taufik, the concrete monster overlooking *kibbutz* Tel Katzir, would be an exercise in alpinism under artillery fire, but the soldiers and officers who had to take part in this operation were lucky. They were ready but did not know what the Chief of Staff knew. As a result of the action in the north the entire Syrian front had collapsed. Guns were being spiked, positions abandoned, arms thrown away. Syrian troops were crossing into Jordan in their thousands. A long line of buses was also observed speeding towards Damascus from Qnaitra indicating the Syrians were leaving the plateau altogether. The air force did some more dive bombing, the infantry followed the tanks but the positions did not answer the Israeli fire. The southern sector fell without fighting. The settlers ran out from their shelters to embrace the soldiers.'

The battle may have cost the defenders as many as 5,000 casualties including 550 prisoners. The Israelis gave their losses as 115 killed and 306 wounded. In addition the Syrians lost at least fifty tanks, many of them intact, besides a tremendous quantity of artillery, about half of it undamaged.[94]

How did Brigadier-General Elazar manage to break through this formidable position in twenty-seven hours?

---

[94] The Syrians had 'a considerable number of brand new Russian 130mm guns which have a range of 16 miles, with the date 1966 stamped on their casings'. In addition to their artillery they had the Russian Katyusha. 'Each vehicle carries 12 rockets on a launcher and is capable of firing 24 rockets per minute.' Their range is 10 miles and they have a 10–12lb warhead. General Elazar thought they were not particularly accurate but had a good area effect. (Churchill, p. 182.)

It was, of course, partly a question of morale, and of leadership. The Israelis were spoiling for a fight with the Syrians, who, despite their massive preparations, were not altogether in good order. An Israeli paratrooper gave an account of one of their camps which is revealing as to their interior economy and, therefore, their discipline: 'Compared to the Jordanian camps, where their former British training was evident, the Syrian camps were all filthy. We could find no food — nothing but chocolate and perfume, masses of Eau de Cologne. Even in their tanks they had chocolate and Eau de Cologne. They had very nasty cigarettes, much inferior to the Jordanian ones. But they had very good dates. We came to a dug-out which had obviously been occupied by a couple of officers as there were two mattresses in it. One of them stank so badly that we burnt it. It was a very difficult job, it kept on going out and smouldered for a long time — the smell was disgusting.'[95] Clearly the frequent purges of the Syrian officer corps had left them with low standards in matters of discipline. At the same time Israeli assault troops described some of the men as 'fighting like tigers'.

The day and night pounding from the air which began on 8 June was certainly a decisive factor, for although some of the Syrian bunkers had so much concrete that 1,000lb bombs could not pierce them, the lack of sleep was bound to sap the defenders' morale in the long run. 'By the Saturday morning the Syrians were running from their bunkers.'[96] *En passant* it is interesting to learn that the bunkers were 'designed with overhanging lips' to keep out napalm,[97] though exactly how this was achieved does not appear.

---

[95] Churchill, p. 189.
[96] Churchill, p. 182.
[97] Churchill, p.182.

It was not easy for General Elazar to achieve surprise, though he was able to form up under cover of darkness. All he could do was to draw attention to his centre (the Korazim sector) by way of a feint, while attacking on the flanks. The helicopter assault by paratroopers, allotted to Brigadier-General Elad Peled's[98] command on the southern flank, was sufficiently novel to surprise the Syrians, especially as the assault came in from the rear. But this happened on the 10th when the Syrian position had already been broken.

The worst fighting was on the northern flank of the position. At Kfar Szold the Israeli battle group attacked up a steep slope, always harder to defend than a gradual one since there is bound to be 'dead ground' which the defenders cannot see into. Well to the fore were unarmoured bulldozers. Needless to say the engineers suffered heavily and so did the officers, but nevertheless the break-in was achieved. Lack of air cover probably discouraged the Syrians from laying on any serious counter-attack. Without one it was certain that the Israelis would gradually eat their way into the position where, as it turned out, there were not separate lines as in Sinai or the French Maginot, but a continuous zone of mutually-supporting bunkers.

The Syrians cannot be said to have managed their affairs very skilfully. Their only — and very minor — offensive movements were made *after* their air force had been crippled. The heavy, and evidently somewhat inaccurate shelling of the

---

[98] He had already captured Jenin and pushed on to take Nablus, from the rear (7 June). In 1948 he had relieved Safad, rescuing the orthodox Jewish colony and leading to the saying, 'Safad was saved by an action and a miracle. The action was that the orthodox prayed all day. The miracle was that a platoon of the Palmach arrived in the evening.' Peled was the commander of the National Defence College in Jerusalem when I visited it in 1966.

first four days infuriated the Israelis without causing them serious damage in the military sense. Seeing what had happened to the Egyptians this was surely asking for trouble. It seems likely that the Syrians were slow to appreciate the full extent of the disaster to their allies.

Through the ages fortifications have had a fascination for military commanders, and it must be conceded that in some cases they have been very effective. An obvious case is Wellington's famous Lines of Torres Vedras — in country not unlike that of Galilee. But Wellington manned his forts — except for the key position above Sobral — with militia and kept his field army under his hand. The Syrians certainly kept a mobile reserve, though part of it may have been intended to overawe Damascus. But deprived of air cover the armour was ineffective in its efforts to drive out the Israelis who had penetrated their forward positions. What is the conclusion? Is it that in modern war no fortress is impregnable? It may be so, yet we have the examples of Stalingrad and Leningrad, of Imphal and Kohima to consider. The ancient rules hold good it seems, and they may be summarized by saying that forts and fortresses are only useful in conjunction with a field army; and that the general who puts his field army into a fortress is like the man, who, when his ship is sinking, lays a firm hold of the anchor.[99] Certainly in these days of air photography, napalm and helicopter landings a fortified line is somewhat suspect. The enterprising commander will endeavour to keep his army mobile and look for opportunities for offensive action.

With air cover gone to sit in a position like that covering Qnaitra or El Arish, however carefully fortified, is to put your

---

[99] Cf. Hamley's *Operations of War*. Sir John French admitted — somewhat naively — that it was his recollection of this adage that prevented his throwing the B.E.F. into Maubeuge in 1914.

head beneath the guillotine. It only remains for the blade to descend.

CHAPTER XI CHRONOLOGY

9 June 1967: President Nasser broadcasts his resignation.

10 June 1967: President Nasser withdraws his resignation. Cease-fire comes into force.

12 June 1967: Inter-Arab conference at Kuwait. President Boumédiène of Algeria visits Moscow.

17 June 1967: President Kosygin arrives in Washington.

20 June 1967: Soviet fleet arrives in Alexandria.

21–24 June 1967: President Podgorny of U.S.S.R. visits Cairo.

23–25 June 1967: Kosygin-Johnson Summit at Goldboro, U.S.A.

26 June 1967: King Hussein addresses United Nations.

4 July 1967: U.N. General Assembly fails to carry any resolution on the Middle East.

10 July 1967: Security Council agrees to place observers on Canal.

11–12 July 1967: East European Summit on Middle East.

16–18 July 1967: Presidents of Egypt, Syria, Algeria, Iraq and Sudan meet in Cairo.

17 July 1967: U.N. Observers take up positions. Presidents Boumédiène and Arif in Moscow.

1–6 August 1967: Arab foreign ministers confer at Khartoum to find basis for Summit Meeting.

15 September 1967: Suicide of Field-Marshal Abdul Hakim Amer.

CHAPTER XI: THE POWERS IN DISARRAY

The tumult and the shouting dies...

The call for a cease-fire came and in their own good time the Israelis heard it — but not before Syria too had been smitten hip and thigh.

Throughout the world, civilized men and women, wondering by how much World War Three had been averted, welcomed the return of normality — whatever that meant in 1967. Many, if they were honest, would have admitted to twinges of regret. For a week, the world had been moved by emotions it had forgotten since 1945, bellicose emotions which strategic commentators, those Fabians of the nuclear age, had warned it were now too dangerous to indulge. To watch their discomfiture had been one of the war's vicarious pleasures. Their theories of 'graduated deterrence' and 'controlled response' had never meant much to a respectful public; it was gratifying to discover how much less to the victorious Israelis.

But as the adrenalin ebbed slowly from the world's bloodstream, the sensations of the ringside gave way to more sombre mood. What had those six fierce days cost in blood and treasure, and in the misery of non-combatants?

In Russian tanks and French aeroplanes, the score did not altogether defy computation. The Arabs had lost the bulk of their armour: 800 of Egypt's tanks and assault guns were gone, 150 of Jordan's 250, 50 of Syria's 300. Egypt had lost all but 160 of her 500 planes, the majority to ground attack but 40 in one-sided dogfights, Syria 40 of her 110, Jordan all her 25 ageing Hunters. Israel admitted losses of 40 among her 300 planes, many ground-attack trainers downed by ack-ack, rather than expensive interceptors or fighter-bombers. She had actually added to her tank park some 200 Russian T-54s, and T-55s and American Pattons. None of these had done as well as her own mainstay, the Centurion with its 105mm gun, whose performance had gladdened the hearts of British arms salesmen. But this booty would perhaps allow the Israelis to pension off at last their doughty 'Super' Shermans of 1943 vintage.

Israel's high command admitted the loss of 679 killed and 2,563 wounded up to 11 June, a fraction of her casualties in 1948, when she lost almost 6,000, but three times those of 1956. Now as then an undue proportion, 23 per cent, represented officers, schooled to order 'follow me'. Overall, the fatal casualty rate touched just .25 per cent of her mobilized manpower but one even as low as that is hard for such a tiny nation to bear. By comparison with Jordan's, however, it is insignificant. Her losses have been put as high as 15,000 killed with four out of nine brigades destroyed. Syrian casualties amounted to some 5,000 — almost all in a single day. Iraq's are unknown; but her expeditionary force did not escape hurt in encounters at H3 or around Jenin. Egypt's losses, still apparently concealed from its public, were catastrophic. In military reckoning, seven of her divisions were destroyed; in human terms, perhaps 15,000 of her men were killed or died of privation. The Israelis accepted as prisoners only the higher ranks; the *simples soldats* were left, with what water could be spared, to find their own way home across the wastes. Many failed to arrive.

Perhaps the outstanding casualty of the Sinai campaign was Field Marshal Abdul Hakim Amer, who was dismissed by President Nasser, his friend of 30 years, and following an abortive army plot to reinstate him, committed suicide rather than be 'questioned' as to its ramifications.

Hakim Amer was born in 1919 and after training, as Nasser did, at the Military Academy in Cairo, was commissioned in 1939. He passed the Staff Officers' College in 1948, and fought with some distinction in the first of the three campaigns against Israel. He and Nasser were leaders of the Free Officers' Movement which overthrew King Farouk in 1952. Thereafter his promotion was rapid. He became Director of General Neguib's office at the presidency, and by 1953 had risen to major-general. He was 34. He was commander-in-chief of the Egyptian armed forces (1953–1958) and of those of the U.A.R. (1958–1962). He was governor of Syria from 1959 until the break up of the U.A.R. in 1961. Thereafter he rose to be Minister of War and first vice-president. It is not impossible that his reputation may have suffered in Nasser's eyes due to the failure to destroy the Royalists in the Yemen.

Some 50 Egyptian Army officers, thought for the most part to have been Amer's men, were dismissed at the same time as the Field-Marshal. It was his opinion that the position in Sinai was untenable once the Israelis had robbed the Egyptian Army of effective air cover. Not unnaturally his supporters preferred this view to the notion that the Army was to blame, because its officer corps was not up to the work. In reality both factors were important.

The Germans from 1943 to 1945, as well as the Viet Cong, have both shown that it is possible to operate without effective air cover, but neither was faced with the problem of doing so in a desert devoid of cover. Amer's friends brooded under a sense of injustice. Soon they were plotting to reinstate their chief by force. However their plot seems to have lacked the subtlety, resolution and ruthlessness demanded of such an operation. According to *Al Ahram*, the newspaper generally regarded as the President's mouthpiece, it was planned to execute the plot on the night of 27 August. But — presumably due to some lack of security on the part of the conspirators — Field-Marshal Amer was placed under house arrest 24 hours beforehand.

It seems that Shamsuddin Badran, a former War Minister, was to be Prime Minister. Hakim Amer's other confederates included a former Minister of the Interior, Abbas Radwan, and a former chief of the intelligence service, Salah Nasr. The revolution council was to have included two former major-generals, Galal Haridi and Osman Nassar. The latter had been cashiered for deserting his brigade in Sinai. The Air Force was represented by Group Captain Tahsin Zaki.

It is obvious that the Sinai campaign had left the Egyptian officer corps bitter and discontented with the role of Nasser's scapegoat, and although the plot failed it was symptomatic of a malaise which it would take many years to root out. Hakim Amer was unquestionably one of Egypt's foremost soldiers, and, though that may seem faint praise, his disgrace and death were bound to cause unrest. In the long run the loss of such a pillar of his regime can hardly be an advantage to Nasser.

The Sinai fiasco was of Nasser's own contriving. The attempt to place the burden of blame on other shoulders may in time prove too transparent even for an Egyptian public mesmerized by its leader's eloquence.

The most pitiful victims were civilian. The war of 1948 had displaced several hundred thousand Palestinian Arabs. They and their progeny in Gaza or West Jordan numbered at this war's outbreak over 700,000. The week's fighting and its aftermath impelled 100,000 of those in West Jordan camps and another 100,000 from its towns and villages to leave their homes. On 30 June they were still crossing the semi-demolished Allenby Bridge into East Jordan at the rate of 5,000 a day, taking with them only what they could carry. Their flight brought down a barrage of charge and counter-charge between victors and vanquished. It was alleged that many had been told by Israeli soldiers to 'go to Hussein' and that they had been harried on their way. Israel insisted that, as in 1948, many had been scared into flight by the Arab radio. This was irrelevant to their plight which the world soon knew to be extreme. 'At the Jordan Government Wadi Dhi Lel camp on the Mafraq road north of Amman,' reported John Mossman in the *Daily Telegraph*, 10 August, 'which accommodates 11,500 refugees in tents, I saw hundreds of children playing on rotting refuse heaps. They are all underfed. The water supply is hardly enough for 1,000. There are no latrines. One doctor told me "It is surprising there is not a serious epidemic, yet. But when the wet cold winter sets in I am horrified to think of the disease and suffering there will be." A British doctor and those nurses of the Save the Children Fund are fighting a losing battle at the Camp. One day, when the Government did not supply the usual one hot meal, the Save the Children Fund stepped in with a ration of cheese. Each of the 2,000 children who queued for lunch received only one piece of cheese the size of a matchbox. At least two-thirds of the refugees in the camp are children, women, many of whom are pregnant, and old people: the able bodied men are still on the West Bank, in the army or are touring Jordan looking for work. Thousands of families have been split by the war. Many wage-earning men who are in Jordan cannot get money to them or even see them at the Allenby Bridge.' Mossman reported that 'Israeli troops immediately suppress attempts by families to shout messages to each other across the Jordan River'. By the end of July, the Israeli Government had in fact agreed to allow genuine residents of the West Bank to return, and an overwhelmed Jordan was anxious that they should. But Red Cross Observers estimated that all but 30,000 were too fearful to do so. The formalities returnees had to complete were, in any case, exacting and Israel refused to extend the closing date for repatriation beyond 31 August. The burden of re-settlement, relief and military occupation must have indeed looked daunting. But unless Israel shoulders them, the plight of the refugees will provide an insurmountable obstacle to the finding of a *modus vivendi*, let alone a reconciliation with her neighbours.

The war's impact on the losers' economies, compounded as it was by their masochistic policies of embargo, ranged from the very grave to the disastrous. Jordan, quite simply, is ruined. She already depended upon foreign subsidies — British, American and Arab — to maintain the machinery of government. She has now lost the most productive half of her country, which brought her $12m annually in tourist revenue alone. The Amman hotel proprietor who told a BBC interviewer that 'Of course we will fight for Jerusalem. It is our bread and butter' no doubt exaggerated in suggesting that the Arabs would resume — let alone win — the war, but as a statement of hard commercial fact he spoke nothing but the truth. Egypt has cut off her nose to spite her face. The closure of the canal, hostility to western tourists and oil embargo lose her about £12½m a month, almost as much as her cotton exports bring her and about half her annual foreign currency earnings. Her development budget for 1967–8 has been cut from £350m to £250m and will probably be cut again. She like

Jordan has become, temporarily at least, a remittance state. Indeed, without interim loans of £35m from other Arab States, it is difficult to see how her economy could have borne up as it has. The prospect of emancipation from her single crop economy has further receded.

The victor reckons to break even — perhaps, a current Tel Aviv joke has it, to make a small profit. The war cost Israel £200m. Pledges of gifts by World Jewry have already almost covered the outlay. To this windfall should be added the value of the modern Soviet equipment captured on the battlefields and, who knows, to be shown for a fee to the C.I.A. But it will cost at least £2m a month to maintain living standards among the Arabs of the occupied areas and £20m a month to keep even half the army mobilized, which while Arab intransigence persists she cannot avoid doing. Victory, moreover, seems to have solved neither of Israel's pre-war economic problems — very slow growth and high unemployment rates, and an unfavourable trade balance. Expanded tourism will help to offset her foreign deficit — at Jordan's expense. Only a new influx of immigrants would solve the former problems. It is difficult to see whence they would come. Certainly neither from Russia or America, the last great centres of dispersion.

The Israelis are not unnaturally reticent as to the extent to which they have kept their army mobilized. By European standards the Armies of Occupation might be expected to number as much as a third of their potential strength. That is to say something like 10 brigades or brigade groups. The Syrians used to keep at least five brigades in their 'Maginot'. It would perhaps be surprising if the Israelis could face so unpredictable an opponent with less than two brigades. Considering the importance of the occupied Jordanian territory one can hardly imagine that there would be less than a brigade in the Jerusalem area and another in Nablus district. With outposts on the Suez Canal one supposes that Sinai calls for at least a division, besides a garrison for hostile Gaza. That could easily account for four more brigades. Add the regular paratroop brigade as a mobile reserve — partly helicopter-borne — and you have a total of nine brigades. This is mere speculation, but, although the Israelis make a practice of holding their Forward Defended Localities with very light forces, it would be surprising if the total could be cut much below nine brigades. However, the Israelis have strong economic reasons for wishing to demobilize, and, given their excellent intelligence and their first-rate mobilization scheme, it is likely that they have demobilized far beyond the point which British or American commanders, similarly placed, would consider prudent.

No doubt they have redeployed their regular units, so that they are now in Syrian, Jordanian or Egyptian camps and positions. At the moment they can afford to leave Israel itself but thinly garrisoned. Even so one would suppose that Israel's regular forces are hardly sufficient to hold down all the occupied territory.

This was the balance sheet. Victors and vanquished took stock with varying degrees of realism and adjusted their policies accordingly. Not without discord. Israeli doves and hawks seemed as little agreed on the disposal of the fruits of war as they had been on the balance of its risks a few weeks before Jerusalem was declared by acclaim 'liberated territory' and the Old City incorporated within the New as a single municipality. The future of the 'occupied territories' — West Jordan, Gaza and the Syrian heights — was not to be arranged so simply. General Dayan seemed to believe that they should become national territory but admitted that this opinion was personal and unofficial. It lent weight to rumours of a struggle for power within the government. David Ben Gurion spoke only of the West Bank's autonomous association with Israel. Eshkol, Eban and the Cabinet moderates were silent on annexations. Their view, like that of all Israelis, seemed to be that the security of their frontiers must be assured and that, pending a settlement, the I.D.F. would stand on the cease-fire lines. It was made clear that they would prefer a settlement direct with the Arab States, not one imposed or guaranteed by the powers or by U.N.O., whose offices they had learnt to mistrust.

The Arabs made it equally clear that they would not move jot or tittle from their stance of non-recognition. Indeed, if foreign policy pronouncements were all the world had to go by, it might have thought the Arabs defeated by phantoms. Try as they might, however, they could not quite disguise the fact of defeat from themselves. Inevitably, it had repercussions. The most dramatic, if short lived, was Nasser's resignation, announced on 9 June, withdrawn by popular protest the following day. What part Nasser's political machine had played in organizing the tumult of demands for second thoughts is unclear. It undoubtedly strengthened his hand for the purge of military commanders which followed his resumption of power. But he did not quite manage to conjure up a martyr's crown, as he had done in 1956. That in 1967 went to King Hussein of Jordan, who had come to Egypt's aid almost unbidden and been seen to go down fighting. He, alone among Arab leaders, emerged from the war with his position stronger at home and his image improved abroad. His modesty and evident distress won him sympathy wherever his round of visits took him in the following weeks: from General de Gaulle, the Pope, the

General Assembly. But, as he knew only too well, neither Western nor Arab sympathy would help him forward the only policy which made sense for Jordan — an accommodation with Israel. Though he hinted at its desirability, he dared not risk an overture.

The Arab States which would hold him true to the common policy of non-recognition of Israel proved to have difficulty, however, in finding other grounds for agreement in the weeks which followed the collapse of the Holy War. The old divisions soon reappeared. President Boumédiène of Algeria was quick to assert that the Arabs had 'lost a battle but not the war' and talked of its prosecution by revolutionary methods. The other 'revolutionary' states — Egypt, Iraq and Syria — equally took this line. And a strategy of augmented guerrilla activity against Israel has obvious attractions and even a certain plausibility, particularly when advocated by the victor of the national struggle with France. It would be as well to remember, however, that the French army had come very close to suppressing all resistance within Algeria at the moment when de Gaulle decided to concede. The I.D.F. is not a whit less efficient and plays for higher stakes. The princely Arab States certainly showed no taste for such a dangerous undertaking.

Indeed, it soon became clear that they found the consequences of making common cause with their 'revolutionary' brothers both uncomfortable and pointless. It was they who had to keep their oil off the market — not Egypt (whose few oil wells were in Israeli hands and just supplying her domestic needs) nor Algeria. This embargo did not hurt Israel. It caused some irritation in Europe, costing British buyers a small surcharge and making necessary contingency plans for rationing, but it did no 'imperialist' fundamental harm. It damaged the economies of Saudi Arabia, Libya and

Iraq very considerably. Moreover, it gladdened Russia. Both results were displeasing to the princes, who have use for the lost revenues and no time for communism.

Two other Arab leaders manifested impatience with the prevailing policy of immobility. Bourguiba of Tunisia, perhaps the most occidental and certainly the most firmly-seated head of state in the Arab World, found it wholly sterile and argued for a long term policy 'based on pressures and concessions to break the opponent' — clear evidence of his belief that Israel is here to stay. King Hassan of Morocco showed some signs of sharing his view.

But the Arab conservatives could not wholly ignore public opinion at home. This was as pan-Arab as ever and even more anti-Israeli. Hence their ready participation in a round of international conferences — in Kuwait on 17 June and in Khartoum between 1–6 August. Little enough came of them. It even seemed for a time that the delegates at Khartoum would fail to find a basis for the Arab Summit meeting scheduled for mid-August, since Saudi Arabia made its attendance conditional on Egypt's agreement to withdraw her troops from the Yemen. At the last moment, however, Premier Mahgoub of the Sudan appeared to have found a formula acceptable to both: the supervision of a plebiscite by an inter-Arab force, of the sort which had seen the Iraq-Kuwait crisis through in 1961. But no Arab leader can approach the Summit with much optimism. The conservatives are suspicious of the progressives' stubborn determination to entangle the Arab World more deeply with Russia. The progressives fear to find themselves outvoted. Both parties best hopes lie in the mediatory skills of Premier Mahgoub, who has emerged as a leader of wisdom and stature, and may well move to the secretaryship of the Arab League.

Russia's response to the humiliation of her Arab protégés was throughout confused. Her evident unwillingness to confront America in the Middle East had hardly added to her stock of good-will in the area. But she showed herself anxious to hang on to what advantages she still enjoyed there and her clients could hardly spurn what shreds of support she continued to proffer. These came in two kinds: arms and words. On 26 June, Cairo International Airport was closed at one hour's notice and the first consignments of a Russian airlift of equipment began. It was estimated that by mid-July, about half the aircraft and a quarter of the tanks lost by the Arab armies had already been replaced. What stiffening of morale or confidence in their tactical methods the Soviets will manage to restore is a matter for speculation.

In public utterances the Russians were at first very fierce. On 9 June, representatives of six East European States, including Yugoslavia, met in Moscow to condemn America of collusion with Israel. Rumania declined to sign. But when next they met, 11–12 July, their pledges of support for their Arab socialist friends were notably more tepid. One of the reasons undoubtedly was the realization of the growing cost of this friendship. Boumédiène, who had visited Moscow on 12 June, and was to do so again with Arif on 17 July, appears to have asked for a good deal more than re-equipment and displays of strength (a Russian fleet of 19 warships anchored in Alexandria harbour on 20 July). They seem to have expected Russia to indemnify the Arabs for the cost of the oil and trade embargo. It would be surprising if Russia were willing to throw more good money after so much bad. She as yet shows no signs of doing so. All the evidence, indeed, points to a decision to swallow some pride and make what accommodation she can with America. The Glassboro Summit meetings between Johnson and Kosygin on 23 and 25 June brought forth little agreement but a great deal of cordiality. It seems to have been a good deal more successful, as meetings go, than President Podgorny's with Nasser in Cairo, 21–24 June.

America has throughout been careful to avoid taking sides or giving offence. Inevitably she has done so. There is little any aggrieved party can do about it. She is immune from the effects of the embargo. She has proved that she can outface Russia. She is potentially a more generous source of aid, which she is clearly not unwilling to grant if the Arabs will meet her halfway. And although she will not countenance policies destructive of Israel's integrity, she will not give the Arabs the satisfaction of championing her cause at their expense. Her basic aims, in fact, are incorporated in the five points laid down by President Johnson on 19 June: (i) the right of each nation's existence; (ii) a just settlement of the refugee problem; (iii) respect of maritime rights; (iv) a limitation of the Middle Eastern arms race; and (v) the preservation of territorial integrity. What this would mean in reality is that the Arabs should recognize Israel and provide copper bottomed guarantees of her immunity from further attack, while she in return should withdraw from her captured possessions and resettle or compensate those Arabs displaced by this war and that of 1948. The powers should meanwhile starve both sides of arms. The Canal and the Straits of Tiran should be open to the ships of all nations. As policies go, it is unrealistically ambitious. The Americans would be the first to concede that this was so, and are right to stand on all of it in the hope of bringing parts to fruition.

Where her vital interests are concerned, America has come well out of the crisis. The princely states, in which she has such enormous sums invested (Aramco represents half U.S. foreign holdings) have been alienated not at all by her stand and are clearly unconvinced by the progressives' charges of collusion between her and Israel. And at no time did Russia look like making a Cuban style confrontation of their differences.

The United Nations has neither gained nor lost influence. It has signally failed to muster international agreement on the future of Israel and its neighbours. The General Assembly spent over a month searching for a formula. It was able to pass a Swedish resolution appealing for relief funds, and a Pakistani appeal to Israel to leave unchanged the status of Jerusalem. It was unable to pass any of six resolutions presented on 4 July and designed to accelerate a settlement between the belligerents. A Yugoslav proposal which called on Israel to withdraw to the 1948 armistice lines and a Latin American which wanted to further an Arab abandonment of the 'state of belligerence', the internationalisation of Jerusalem and the establishment of demilitarized zones came nearest to acceptance but both failed to achieve a two-thirds majority. Israel's policy of aid for the smaller African and Asian States serves her well at voting time in the General Assembly.

To the United Nations' credit must be reckoned the establishment of a cease-fire supervising team. Early in July, fighting broke out sporadically along the Canal. Egypt and Israel each accused the other of violations and from the brouhaha which followed U Thant was able to extract agreement to the stationing of neutral observers on both banks. In the event of an emergency, they will be able to communicate with each other only via New York — at least in strict theory. One suspects that they may find more direct means.

The reactions of two other powers to the crisis deserve note — those of China and President de Gaulle. Both were in their bizarre fashion, predictable. In Peking, on 13 June, Chou Yi, the foreign minister, chose the occasion of the celebration of King Mahendra's birthday at the Nepalese embassy to denounce 'U.S.–British–Soviet collusion'. He accused that 'in line with the attitude and position it has taken with regard to the Vietnam Question, the Soviet revisionists leading clique has once again played the ignominious role of sham supporter but real betrayer of the Arab people in their resistance against the war of aggression waged by U.S. and British imperialism and Israel'. Subsequent Chinese pronouncements have been couched in similar vein; but as earnest of support they have been able to send only a modest shipment of wheat to Egypt. President de Gaulle's assistance was altogether more valuable. He assured the Arab leaders of his help in preventing the distribution of oil from France to countries under their ban and saw to it that French votes were cast wherever they would best help the Arab cause in the United Nations. He also declared that Israel should withdraw from its conquests.

Seismic tremors from the war were felt all over the world, recorded, commented, and sometimes acted, upon. On 10 June, President Nyrere of Tanzania sent fulsome messages to Nasser, first begging him to stay on, then rejoicing at his decision to do so. The *Ghana Evening News* of that day was not for one moment convinced that the U.S. or U.K. had been involved in the conflict. 'Nasser got beaten so far by better organized, better trained and better equipped Israeli forces.' On 12 June, Rhodesian Radio opined that Israel's victory had given the West 'a breathing space in which to realise who its allies really are'. There were numerous reports of Rhodesians volunteering for action in Israel. On 6 June, President Houphouet-Boigny of the Ivory Coast twice received the Israeli ambassador to assure him of his country's 'total support' for Israel. On 14 June, President Hastings Banda of Malawi said that Israel 'did the right thing'. In Chile the Egyptian ambassador, in explaining his government's attitude to the Straits of Tiran, drew an unfortunate parallel with Chile's position vis-à-vis the Argentine in the Magellan and Beagle Straits in Tierra del Fuego. This provoked enquiries from the Argentine, where the Egyptian ambassador was forced to say that his colleague's statement did not reflect his country's attitude to the Chilean–Argentinian dispute.

On 26 June, at a secret consistory in Rome, the Pope created 27 new cardinals. In his speech, he appealed for a rapid solution of the territorial problems of the Middle East, and expressed his profound sadness at the fate of the Palestinian refugees. 'This holy city of Jerusalem,' he went on, 'should remain for ever what it represented, the city of God, a free oasis of peace and prayer, a place of meeting, of elevation and concord for all, with its own status internationally guaranteed.' His was a still, small unheeded voice.

CHAPTER XII: AFTERTHOUGHTS

'Pray for the Peace of Jerusalem' ...

The third and, so far, the briefest of the three campaigns of the Arab-Israeli War for Palestine was over. What did it prove?

Despite events in Goa and the Yemen it may be said that at this period the use of violence to further the ends of state policy was generally condemned among civilized nations. And now one of the smallest sovereign powers in the world had actually defeated its neighbours, overrunning considerable tracts of territory. The superpowers, the United Nations, and the Pope had all alike denounced, or at least deplored, this use of force, but, confident that none of them would actually do anything, the Israelis had continued the campaign until, their immediate aims achieved, they had found it convenient to hear the ceasefire. Fear that the war might spread had compelled the superpowers to tread warily. The United Nations, whose weakness had been exposed even before the campaign began, was incapable of imposing its will on the Israelis.

Although Russian brinkmanship had done so much to bring on the crisis, things had gone much further than the Kremlin had either desired or expected. Her Arab friends had lost a great deal of valuable equipment, but in other respects things had not turned out to the disadvantage of the U.S.S.R.

Russia, one of the first powers to recognize Israel in 1948, had only supported Egypt since 1955 and then only because an occasional Middle East crisis fitted in with her policy of embarrassing the Western Powers, and especially the U.S.A. The interruption of oil supplies to the West had been one advantage gained. Another was that the defeated Arabs, excluding Jordan, now depended upon her more than ever, for who else was to replace their lost planes and tanks? The survival of Israel did not distress the Russians, since without her presence in the midst of the Arab World it would be much more difficult to stir up trouble in the Middle East whenever it should seem appropriate to do so.

As for the U.S.A. the swift Israeli victory, predicted by President Lyndon B. Johnson's military advisors, had come as a great relief. Heavily committed in Vietnam the last thing he wanted was military operations elsewhere. Had the Egyptians won the air battle and followed it up with a serious thrust at Tel-Aviv, the Jews in the U.S.A. would doubtless have compelled Mr. Johnson to intervene. He must have been grateful to the Israelis for saving him from this situation, with all its inherent dangers of a major confrontation with Russia. One of the most interesting features of the campaign was that American military experts were able to predict its outcome with such accuracy, for it was not a case where counting men, tanks and planes — the Military Balance — was much help.

Great Britain as well as the U.S.A. came in for much angry denunciation from the Arab leaders. Israel, they argued, in the bitterness of defeat, had only won because of collusion. Only the intervention of British and American planes could account for the swift destruction of the Arab air forces. This 'monstrous lie', worthy of Hitler himself, was hard to refute. It was no doubt part of the legacy of Suez that Britain should be so unjustly pilloried. It was ironical that France, whose collusion with Israel in 1956 was a matter of history, and who had provided the entire Israeli Air Force, should have contrived to maintain a lofty air of magnanimous neutrality. In

Arab eyes President de Gaulle was reaping the credit for his successful termination of the Algerian War.

It was true that Nasser had shown himself no friend to Britain, but it was inconceivable after the Suez fiasco that a Labour government should rush in where a Conservative one had dared to tread with such unfortunate results. But to convince an emotional and uncritical Arab public of this obvious truth was beyond the wit of the government or the power of the BBC. No doubt the continued presence of British troops in Aden was sufficient to enable the Arab leaders to keep the suspicions of their subjects alive.

The paramount British interest in the Middle East at this period was a commercial one: the need to purchase oil. Britain then depended upon oil for 43 per cent of her fuel. Coal met 55.1 per cent of the demand, atomic energy 1 per cent and natural gas 0.7 per cent. Not before about 1975, it was thought, would atomic energy be able to begin reducing the country's dependence on oil. The purchase of oil, being a purely commercial business, did not necessarily demand a British military presence in the Middle East. A good case could be made for the argument that the *absence* of British forces from this tense area would be a positive advantage.

The freedom of navigation was, of course, a British interest, but one that was common to the other maritime powers, including the U.S.A. and Norway. This could best be handled, albeit slowly, through the U.N.O.

The closure of the Suez Canal, though costly, was less of a calamity than it had been in 1956. The introduction of larger tankers had made it possible to bring great quantities of oil round the Cape, a journey that took them between ten and fifteen days longer than the voyage by the Suez route.

Needless to say, along with other Christian countries, Great Britain had an interest in the safety of the Holy Places in Jordan, especially those in Jerusalem and Bethlehem. These fortunately survived the fighting remarkably well, and were no less accessible to visitors or pilgrims for being in Jewish rather than Moslem care.

The British government was under a certain amount of pressure from British Jewry and from Zionists to support Israel, and on the whole British public opinion was on her side throughout the crisis and the campaign. However a good deal of sympathy was felt for King Hussein of Jordan, and it was not altogether forgotten that Trans-Jordan had remained Britain's ally throughout World War Two. On humanitarian grounds there was a genuine interest in the question of settling the unfortunate Palestine refugees. The wrongs done to Jews in Germany did not provide a legitimate reason for inflicting similar sufferings on innocent Arabs.

When all these considerations had been taken into account and given such weight as they merited, it seemed that Great Britain's paramount interest in the Middle East, at this period, was to be able to purchase what oil she required without interruption.

This, however, was altogether too cynical a view. Israel was, after all, a fellow member of U.N.O. and it could scarcely be accounted either honourable or expedient for Great Britain or any of the other powers to permit her to be devoured. For Great Britain no less than the U.S.A. it was decidedly a relief when Israel's *blitzkrieg* banished, for a time, mental conflicts. But since Act Four had still to be played it behoved the British government to consider where it would stand when next the Arabs should be inspired to proclaim the *Jihad*.

The sad truth was that the odds were very heavily against the third campaign of the Palestine War being its last. There was no likelihood that Russia would wish to see this running sore healed. Nor was there much reason to suppose that the Israelis would quit all, or some, of their territorial gains. The Arab leaders could not afford to sit round the table with their opponents without the recovery of the lost territories and the solution of the refugee problem. These were not circumstances that promised a settlement of any sort, far less a lasting one.

From the military point of view this rather old-fashioned campaign had features of interest. In the first place it was strongly reminiscent of the *Blitzkrieg*, World War Two style. The comparison with the Wavell–O'Connor offensive of 1940–41 has already been noted, but the techniques used seem to have been lifted bodily from the German campaigns of the 1939–41 period, with the destruction of the defender's air force, being followed up by relentless armoured thrusts. The parallels between the Sinai campaigns of 1956 and 1967 are also striking, but the second was both more vigorously opposed and more expertly executed. In its general lines the strategy of the campaign was more or less predictable. To hold forth about the Principles of War, Surprise, Offensive Action, is perhaps somewhat academic. The campaign simply proves that the Israelis with their three divisions and two independent brigades had a thoroughly good plan for dealing with seven Egyptian divisions dug in, Soviet fashion. But the fighting was not won by the Planning Staff, it was won in the desert by units that had been trained to fight day and night, to keep up the momentum; by units which were led from in front by men prepared to use the old commando tactics of deep penetration.

'Thou shalt keep abreast of the technological advances of thine age' is no bad commandment for a General Staff. The

Israelis certainly lived up to it, witness the famous 'dibber' bomb, and the 'hotted-up' Centurions. But it was not only a case of technology. Attention to detail also exercised its influence. Bar-Nun and his frogmen-commando, Arik Sharon and his trench-clearing technique — borrowed from the British Army of 1918 — these when 'the chips are down' are the things that win battles. These, and the ability to fight day and night for three days without let-up, and, above all, the notion that leadership is done from in front, were the keys to victory.

The Egyptian private soldier showed himself staunch enough in defence, but he expects to sleep at night, or if not at least to have a spell of Egyptian P.T. in the afternoon. The Israelis were content to fight non-stop all the way across the Sinai Desert and refresh themselves with a dip in the Suez Canal when they got there.

'In war the moral is to the physical as three is to one', said Napoleon, though no doubt he would have been the first to agree that it was no more than a rough rule of thumb. The 1967 campaign proved once more, if proof were needed, that in war mere numbers count for little. Education, talent, spirit, patriotism — these, thank God, count too. Contrariwise, the more sophisticated the weapons one puts into the hands of unsophisticated soldiers — or airmen — the less impressive are the results.

The Israeli army, though technologically abreast of the age, also knew how to make do with a considerable range of antiques — notably the Sherman tank. There are other armies which might do worse than follow their example. One should strive after the best, but still make use of whatever is available. The British Army does not always do this. As one officer recently (1966) demanded: 'Was it really necessary to have

BAT, MOBAT, WOMBAT and now COMBAT? Do you buy a new dishwasher every year because the advertisers tell you this year's model is fractionally better.' The Israelis in their 1937 pattern web equipment kept their 1967 pattern wits about them. They won not because the Arabs fought badly, but because they fought much better. They showed that for all their manpower the Arabs had a long way to go before they could hope to destroy Israel, especially considering the fact that Russia, while doubtless willing to provide weapons, had no real interest in removing Israel from the Levantine scene.

Still it was not impossible for the Arabs too to learn from the war of 1967. They were quite capable of discerning the value of a pre-emptive strike, and although the fighting had put the frontier *kibbutzim* of the Lake Huleh area outside the range of Syrian artillery, and had denied Jordan the chance to shell Tel-Aviv or New Jerusalem, it was still 9 minutes by jet from Damascus to the crowded city of Tel-Aviv.

There were those who thought that Israel's 1967 *blitzkrieg* had won her ten years' peace, but in fact her strategic position, never brilliant, was only marginally improved, since Air Power was the key to the situation.

Time was on the side of the Arabs if only because there just were not enough Jews in Israel. Even if all the Jews in America should have removed themselves to Zion there would still only be some 8 million in Israel — a population comparable to that of Syria. Lack of immigration spells a decline of economic growth that the modern Sparta, *toujours en vedette*, cannot afford.

With all their good qualities the Israelis, bred in the Sabra cult, had one fault: they were never, or at least seldom, wrong: a difference of opinion with an Israeli was a head-on collision. It may be that the only chance of a settlement was to surrender the territorial gains of 1967 and to solve the complex Palestine refugee problem — possible perhaps with American aid.

It was not to be. Moderates like Eshkol and Eban simply did not have the following to persuade Dayan and Rabin to surrender their hard won gains. So ironically the persecuted Jews of Europe without whom the State of Israel could never have survived the 1948 campaign, by sending a million Arabs into an exile not dissimilar to their own, sowed the seeds of their own destruction.

It was not only in their search for *Lebensraum* that the Israelis proved apt pupils of the Germans. Their very strategy, unconsciously perhaps, went back, via Graf Schlieffen, to King Frederick the Great of Prussia. He too was surrounded by powerful enemies: Austria, Russia, and France. He too, when he felt threatened, reacted with a pre-emptive strike, both in 1740 and in 1756. His instinct taught him to strike at his most dangerous enemy: Austria. Compare Schlieffen's plan to attack first France while holding Russia, and Israel's destruction of the Egyptian army, while holding Jordan and Syria at bay. Frederick thought nothing of seizing an enemy's province, Silesia. Here the comparison is Qnaitra, the West Bank or Sinai, whichever you please. Frederick too fought from a central position, throwing his less mobile enemy off balance by brilliant strokes such as Rossbach and Leuthen (1757). Perhaps the Israelis hoped that just as the Tsarina Elizabeth quit the ranks of Frederick's foes, King Hussein would abandon his republican allies. Perhaps for once History really was repeating herself. But it was strange, even sinister, that the young Zionist state should take Prussia for its model. Still one must not push such comparisons too far.

One can have nothing but admiration for the courage, devotion and efficiency of the Israelis who won the 1967 campaign.

Once again David had defeated Goliath. But this time Goliath, though battered, was still alive.

SELECT BIBLIOGRAPHY

Antonius, George: *The Arab Awakening* (1938).
Barbour, Nevill: *Nisi Dominus* (1946).
Calvacoressi, Peter: *Suez Ten Years After* (1965).
Chatham House (RIIA): *Great Britain and Palestine, 1915–1945* (1946).
Churchill, Randolph S., and Winston S.: *The Six Day War* (1967). Of the short histories published soon after the fighting this is far the best. It is particularly useful for the chronology of events during the actual fighting and, an unusual feature, has a critical analysis of *The BBC Coverage*.
Dayan, Major-General Moshe: *Diary of the Sinai Campaign* (1966). Valuable to anyone wishing to compare the Sinai Campaigns of 1956 and 1967. The Appendix of Operation Orders is of special interest to the student of Military History.
Elston, D. R.: *Israel: The Making of a Nation* (1963).
Glubb, Lieutenant-General Sir John Bagot, KCB, CMG, DSO, OBE, MC: *Britain and the Arabs: A Study of Fifty Years, 1908–1958* (1959).
Ibid.: *The Middle East Crisis: A Personal Interpretation* (1967).
Institute for Strategic Studies: *The Military Balance, 1966–1967*, September 1966.
Ibid.: Figures released to the Press on 6 June 1967.
Ibid.: *The Military Balance, 1967–1968*, as at 31 July 1967.
Kerr, Malcolm: *The Arab Cold War* (1965).
Lenczowski, George: *The Middle East in World Affairs* (1966).
Mansfield, Peter: *Nasser's Egypt* (1965).
Partner, Peter: *Political Guide to the Arab World* (1960).

Sykes, Christopher: *Crossroads to Israel* (1965).
Ibid.: *Two Studies in Virtue* (1953).
Thomas, Hugh: *The Suez Affair* (1966).
Vatikiotis, Professor P. J.: *Politics and the Military in Jordan: A Study of the Arab Legion, 1921–1957* (1967).
Young, Lt.-Colonel Peter: *Bedouin Command* (1956). Describes the life of a Bedouin Regiment (1953–1956) and has an account of the Jerusalem Incident of 1954.

ACKNOWLEDGEMENTS

The first debt I have to acknowledge is to the late Colonel Robert Henriques, whom I first knew when I served on the planning staff of Combined Operations H.Q. in 1942. It was he that invited me to Israel last October and accompanied me everywhere from Dan to Eilat. Thanks to his good offices I was introduced to many people I could not otherwise have hoped to meet, including, among others, Generals Dayan, Rabin and Weizman. In addition I was thoroughly briefed in the H.Q. of the Israel Defence Force, and was enabled to visit many different military establishments.

I wish to express my gratitude to various correspondents in Israel who have sent me information and their comments. These include Arie Hashavia, Lt.-Colonel Elhannan Orren, Maier Asher and Gershon Epstein.

In this country Professor S. E. Finer, a friend of 33 years' standing, gave me the benefit of his knowledge not only of the political set-up in Israel, but of the emotions that the recapture of Jerusalem must arouse in Jewry.

Brigadier Z. Zamir, the Israeli Defence Attaché,c has kindly provided me with maps and much information.

I have to thank Bernard Thorold for helping me to collect information at a time when it seemed a new history of the 'war' was coming from the press every day.

Miss Rifai of the Jordan Embassy kindly attempted to answer my questions as to the effect of events upon her country. I am grateful to her also for arranging for me to be received by His Majesty King Hussein during his recent visit to London.

My colleague John Keegan has given me a great deal of assistance in the preparation of certain chapters, and in reading, and in commenting upon the rest, has placed me very much in his debt.

The staff of the Institute for Strategic Studies gave me a great deal of help, especially with the chapter on the Military Balance. Their efficiency and courtesy is much appreciated.

My wife, at a time of year when it is possible that she would have preferred to bask on the Riviera, typed the MS. She has my thanks, and, no doubt, your sympathy.

A NOTE TO THE READER

If you have enjoyed this book enough to leave a review on **Amazon** and **Goodreads**, then we would be truly grateful.
Sapere Books

Sapere Books is an exciting new publisher of brilliant fiction and popular history.

To find out more about our latest releases and our monthly bargain books visit our website:
saperebooks.com

Printed in Great Britain
by Amazon